# FRIENDS

## OF CHILDREN WITH SPECIAL NEEDS

*Building a Dream Community*

*compiled and edited by*

## JAMES CHIAO

Friends of Children with Special Needs
Building a Dream Community

©2021 FCSN

print ISBN: 978-1-66780-497-2
ebook ISBN: 978-1-66780-498-9

# CONTENTS

# FOREWORD

On a December morning in 1976, my wife woke me up and said, "It is time to go to the hospital." My diary captured some moments in the next 72 eventful hours.

> "The obstetrician gave our baby a score of 9 on the Apgar scale, meaning he is in very good condition." A day later, "Dr. Mills and I sat down besides Margaret's bed, and he told us that several doctors have examined the baby and believe that he has Down Syndrome… When we were alone, Margaret started to weep. We comforted each other and agreed that we could cope with the challenge, that life with Raymond would be full and good." "I decided to call parents in Taiwan again. Their phone was busy the entire evening. I knew that they were calling relatives and friends about having a new grandson… The call was brief for tears rushed out for the first time in my adult life … Afterward, I had a good cry. I felt better. I know that I will never cry for Raymond again." Another day later, "At 6am Dr. Mills called to say that Raymond needed blood transfusion in intensive-care nursery …12 hours later, Raymond needed another transfusion…. another…there is a hole in his heart…"

Having a child with developmental disability is hard for parents, at the moment of diagnosis and during decades of caring for the child's physical and mental disabilities. The hardest part is perhaps not-knowing what's ahead, what her life will be like, what happens to him after the parents pass away.

We also keep wondering how hard it is to be that child. This is not to say that we think the child cannot have a happy life. Raymond likes to say smugly, "I am disabled, but I also have abilities." But I know that he has very hard times, too.

This book is a story about a few persons striking sparks and 10 families lighting a kindling and inviting the community to build a bonfire. Today, this bonfire is illuminating the ways and making lives better for hundreds of children and adults with special needs and their families at three sites in the Southeast San Francisco Bay Area.

Perhaps more importantly, this book, especially the early chapters, is also a guidebook for building the bonfire. It is best, perhaps necessary, to build the bonfire with strong parent involvement, and therefore best done locally.

Chapter 2, The Dream Project, lays out the key concepts. The special-needs citizens should have, beyond their immediate families, a small community where they are respected, loved, and fully accepted. This small community is not a replacement for, but a buffer to the community at large. They live in both communities and can each choose how to divide their time between the two. This small community reminds me of the African proverb "It takes a village to raise a child."

Like a village, this community needs community space and structures for learning, playing, and being together. Some special-needs adults may require residential facility in this community, where they can grow old with friends and dignity. If public and private financial support is the life blood of this community, one can say that parents serving as board members and part-time executives are the heart and brain, and paid staff are the bones and muscles. One mustn't forget the community volunteers; they are friends from the larger community to our children.

This story is ongoing. The community started with Chinese American families. Laudably, its staff, clients and board have become multi-ethnic. The transition of leadership and culture from the first-generation parents to a younger generation of parents (of the younger children) is in progress and appropriately gradual. All signs suggest that the community will navigate through this challenge, perhaps the hardest test for its longevity, as it has done so many times before.

One may hope that, with the help of this book (and perhaps its future updates) and an online network of dream builders, thousands of bonfires will shine in the US and throughout the world one day for children with special needs.

Chenming Hu
FCSN Parent, Board Member 2010-2018, Chair 2016-2018
TSMC Distinguished Professor Emeritus
University of California, Berkeley

# PREFACE

Friends of Children with Special Needs (FCSN) was founded by ten Chinese American families in 1996, with the mission to help children and adults with special needs and their families to find love, hope, respect, and support through integrated community involvement. In the beginning, we met at each other's homes and planned our activities. Within a year, our membership had increased to over fifty families. In 2000, we initiated the Dream Project to build a model community for our special children; and twenty years later, the Dream Project is still considered a success story for the special needs community in the Bay Area. Today, FCSN has grown to over one thousand family members, serving over two hundred and fifty adults, and hundreds more children and families in the Bay Area.

The idea of publishing a book about FCSN is not new. I remember in 2006, Cherene Wang, then FCSN newsletter editor, once asked us if there was any interest in writing a book about FCSN. At the time, we were hesitant about the book because our organization was still young, the people involved were modest, and the fact that the story was complicated involving many individuals and families. However, earlier this year, with twenty-five years under our belt and FCSN in its adulthood, I felt the time was ripe for such an undertaking.

My idea for a book was quite simple: Instead of writing a book about FCSN, we could tell FCSN's story by compiling the articles already published in various FCSN newsletters. We could arrange them in chronological order, with the articles divided into chapters that represent the distinct periods in our history. Because of the length of the book, I was limited to pick articles that are directly related to our development as an organization which mainly came from the presidents, key staff, reporters, and a few volunteers. Many excellent personal articles from parents and volunteers and those in Chinese were set aside, and they must wait for a possible second book.

In the first two years, FCSN was governed by a "Planning Committee", led by Shiow-Luan Chen, Linmei Chiao, and Peter Hsia. In June 1998, the first board of directors was elected by its members. In the early years, the board elected a chairperson, who also acted as the president of the organization. Starting in 2005, FCSN president was separately elected by the board. Here are the elected presidents and chairperson over the years.

| Year | President | Chairperson |
|------|-----------|-------------|
| 1998 | Linmei Chiao | Linmei Chiao |
| 1999 | Tsai-Wei Wu | Tsai-Wei Wu |
| 2000 | Lihuei Yao | Lihuei Yao |
| 2001 | Albert Wang | Albert Wang |
| 2002 | Albert Wang | Albert Wang |
| 2003 | Limin Hu | Limin Hu |
| 2004 | Anna Wang | Anna Wang |
| 2005 | Albert Wang | Limin Hu |
| 2006 | James Chiao | Limin Hu & Albert Wang |
| 2007 | Tsai-Wei Wu | Limin Hu |
| 2008 | Tsai-Wei Wu | Limin Hu |
| 2009 | Tsai-Wei Wu | Limin Hu & Albert Wang |
| 2010 | Tsai-Wei Wu | Limin Hu |

| 2011 | Tsai-Wei Wu | Albert Wang |
|------|-------------|-------------|
| 2012 | Tsai-Wei Wu | Albert Wang |
| 2013 | James Chiao | Limin Hu |
| 2014 | James Chiao | Limin Hu |
| 2015 | Yee-Yeen Wang | Albert Wang |
| 2016 | Yee-Yeen Wang | Chenming Hu |
| 2017 | Yee-Yeen Wang, James Chiao | Chenming Hu |
| 2018 | CK Lee, James Chiao | Albert Wang |
| 2019 | CK Lee | Albert Wang |
| 2020 | CK Lee | James Chiao, Yee-Yeen Wang |
| 2021 | CK Lee | James Chiao, Yee-Yeen Wang |

These are the key players who have led FCSN over the past 25 years – they are instrumental to the success of the organization, and their written articles form the backbone of this book. The last twenty-five years has been an amazing journey for the founding families, and FCSN has grown beyond our wildest dreams. When asked about the prospect of our organization before our annual meeting in June 2021, here is what several co-founders had to say:

> (Anna Wang) "It's my dream that new FCSN families / parents share our mission and vision to deliver Happiness to special needs individuals and Peace of Mind to the families for the next one hundred years."

> (Albert Wang) "To be able to solidify our core mission of building family support, forming the "village" that is sustainable. Using our tremendously successful model to help others, either through expansion or support other families to do the same."

> (Linmei Chiao) "I dream of most FCSN people, volunteers, supporters all can benefit and feel accomplished through

FCSN involvements. One of the areas FCSN can further strengthen is our culture, we want to be innovative, efficient, and most importantly be kind. As a team, we need more patience listening to each other, and take more time to care about each other. We also need to better understand and support our wonderful staff and volunteers. There is still so much to do! And I believe we can do it!"

(James Chiao) "We have been running this organization for 25 years. It is time that we have a new generation of leaders. This transition has already begun and will accelerate in the coming years. We encourage all families to participate and make volunteering a way of life. Our goal is building a community for our special children. The need for such a community is only growing stronger, I expect FCSN to expand and serve many more families in the future."

Thanks to the leadership of our current and past Boards, presidents, management team (Sylvia Yeh, Executive Business Director, Lilian Lin, CFO, and Anna Wang, VP), and the tremendous support from the staff, families, and friends, we have built two centers, numerous programs, and most importantly: a community for people with special needs and their families.

Today, we are not content with what we have achieved so far. In fact, at the height of COVID-19 pandemic in 2020, to address the critical shortage of space in East Bay, FCSN Board made a bold decision to pursue a strategy of expansion. In May 2021, FCSN acquired another 17,000sf building in Fremont, which will be renovated to become our future headquarters. This will resolve our urgent need for more office space and classrooms, and the long waiting list – and it could be the beginning of another Dream Project. We look forward to providing more services and integrated community programs to special needs families in the future.

Finally, I would like to thank our Board of Directors for supporting this project, Lilian and her IT team for retrieving old newsletters from our archives, and our present and past newsletter editors: Cherene Wong, Helen Chou, Wei-Jen Hsia, and Ruth Wei, for reviewing the draft and making numerous suggestions. In addition, many thanks to our youth volunteers Ember Hung and Darren Ko, who helped converting the newsletter articles from PDF to Word format. Last but not the least, thanks to my wife Linmei whom I have shared many moments with during this wonderful journey.

James Chiao
FCSN Parent, FCSN Co-founder, Co-chair 2021, past President/Co-president
Adviser, FCSN Voices (FCSN newsletter)

# CHAPTER 1:

# The Early Years
## *(1996-2000)*

In the early 1990s, before FCSN was born, there was a young special education teacher, Shiow-Luan Chen, who was studying for her master's degree at University of Santa Clara. In her spare time, she would visit many Chinese American families of children with special needs and informed them of the latest trends in special education and helped them setting up play groups. On Sundays, she would teach a bible class where special needs children were welcomed. Through her tireless work over a period of five to six years, she had connected with 20+ Chinese families in the South Bay Area. In late 1995, Shiow invited some of these families to her home and first suggested that the special needs families should get organized in order to help themselves. Months passed and nothing happened, most families were busy and over-burdened, and forming a support group was not a priority on their minds.

One of the special needs parents, Linmei Chiao, was intrigued by Shiow's idea. Linmei also studied special ed in graduate school and was once a special ed teacher. She took the initiative and worked with Shiow to organize a formal meeting to launch the idea. Linmei also recognized the need for outside help and invited her best friends to join them. The seminal meeting took place on April 6th, 1996 at Linmei's home, where eighteen families participated. At the meeting, we all agreed to work together to form a support group with the goal of creating an organization; within days, a planning committee was formed, the committee included key members such as Shiow Luan Chen, Linmei/James Chiao, Peter/Sheau-Yin Hsia, Joyce/Stanely Yeh, Amy/Jason Wang, and Teresa Sun. Soon the committee expanded to include Anna Wang, Sufen Wu, and Jennifer Li, with Shiow as the head of the committee.

In spring 1997, with the help from Su-Ti Lin, a social worker, we were able to start a biweekly family gathering at Asian Pacific Family Resource Center (APFRC) in San Jose. Many key families joined FCSN during the first year, such as John Yang & Linda Huang, CK Lee, and Mannching Wang, and we quickly expanded to fifty families. In 1997, Linmei took over the leadership position while Shiow was on maternity leave. In 1998, FCSN members elected the board; and the board elected Linmei as its first chairperson/president. Peter Hsia also played a huge role in the early years.

# FROM THE FOUNDER'S DESK

## Shiow-Luan Chen, Co-founder, Jan 1997

A summer picnic at Linda Vista Park in Cupertino, which was a huge success as we met many new families. This was the first family event organized by FCSN, and it gave us great confidence that we were filling a real need in the community. (1996)

Many years ago, when I first encountered the word "retardation," I was shocked by the meaning it presented to the world. It meant despair, helplessness, shame, death, pesticide, burden, and desertion.

Twenty years later, the term "special need" has replaced "retardation." By creating dreams for the families of children with special needs, we have set the following goals to make the world a safer place for our children, to bring our children into the community, to encourage parents and siblings to share their feelings and experiences with others, to understand Chinese American heritage, to have hope, to be wanted, to contribute to the society, to feel proud, to love and to be loved.

As a special educator and community advocate working with Chinese American families for the past ten years, I often come across many unanswered questions. For example: how does a Chinese American parent express himself during the parent-teacher conference when he is hindered by his lack of fluency in English which is his second language? What should a Chinese American mother explain to the special-education teacher that "independence" has different meaning in Asian culture than in the mainstreamed culture? All these difficulties are derived from the lack of understanding of cultural differences. Do we really know our own culture's disability needs?

- What's our perception toward disability?
- Do we know how the mainstream society views disability?
- When conflict arises, how do we solve it?
- What's our attitude towards disagreement?
- When faced with life's realities, more questions come up.
- What help can parents get when they have difficulty communicating with school systems due to language and culture differences?
- Who can provide more knowledge about specific disabilities in our first language, Chinese?
- Who can we trust to share our feelings with?
- Where is the child with special needs to go when parents are getting old?

All these questions are to be answered by ourselves. We need to join hands together. What we need we have to get for ourselves. We have to make sure we have a future by helping and caring for each other.

Dr. Martin Luther King Jr. once dreamed that one day little black and white children would join hands as brothers and sisters. His dream came true. Today, we see children in the school yard, in the classroom, in the playground, and in the community holding hands and working side by side regardless of their race and color. We are sure the same thing will happen to our children. One day they will be able to hold hands and work by the sides of those without special needs. But this day will not come by itself. We have to work for it. And this organization is the first step towards this goal.

**Shiow organized a Thanksgiving party in conjunction with Sacred Heart Chinese School. After lunch, parents got together for an informal sharing session. (Nov. 1996)**

We celebrated Mother's Day at Asian Pacific Family Resource Center (APFRC) in San Jose, as mothers were the backbone of families and our organization. (May 1997)

The first hour of our bi-weekly family gathering includes educational seminar for parents and classes for children. Here, Anna is teaching a children's class at one of our family gatherings. (Oct. 18, 1997)

**Here, Linmei is teaching a class of young adults at one of our bi-weekly family gatherings. (1997)**

**Youth volunteers have been an important part of our organization from the very beginning. Here is our first group of high school youth volunteers (top left clockwise: Minh, Allen, Tracy, Yumin) at work during one of our family gatherings. (1997)**

# WE HAVE SO MUCH TO BE THANKFUL FOR!

## Linmei Chiao (President 1998-1999), May 1999

**Linmei conducted experimental classes at her home, to demonstrate how parents could teach our own kids in a group setting. This is a precursor to our classes at the biweekly family gathering which started in Spring 1997. (Oct. 1996)**

At FCSN, it's very easy to find things that can touch your heart and make you feel truly thankful. We gave a group of wonderful people! First, I would like to mention the unique dedication of our board and staff members. It's so great to hear the words like "I'll do my best to help, no matter if I am a board member or not." Let's keep this beautiful spirit alive forever.

I also deeply appreciate the diligence from our teachers and volunteers, as well as the commitments from our Youth Club. Furthermore, on behalf of all the families with special children, I would like to express my sincere appreciation to the other half of the FCSN families. They are the real heroes: They are with us simply because they care about us. Their participation and love warm up our hearts and make FCSN so unique among other organizations.

Aside from the internal help, FCSN has also received tremendous support from many outside friends and organizations in the past years. We would like to thank all the invited speakers who offered us valuable information and make our "Hot Topics" seminar series a big success. We thank Asian Pacific Family Resource Center for providing us with such a wonderful facility as our home base. We thank the Resources for Families and Communities for their kind financial support.

We also thank Tzu-Chi Foundation and San Jose Chinese Catholic Community for supporting our yearly activities in many aspects. Moreover, my thanks go to the Saratoga Rotary Club, Protection and Advocacy Inc., Thomas F. White & Company Inc., Chinese news media and TV broadcasting companies at the Bay Area and many other groups or individuals who have offered help to us. Because of them, FCSN is prospering and growing strong. We look forward to continuously working with them in the many years to come.

FCSN has made significant strides since it was founded in 1997. We are proud of what we are and what we can offer the community today.

However, FCSN is still a young organization and that leaves us plenty of room to grow. We are counting on the continued efforts from each one of our members and the help from our friends throughout the community to build the FCSN's future. Let us support and encourage each other as we go forward in building a better quality of lives for our children, and for ourselves in turn.

We held our first Annual Meeting and Family Day at CCC in San Jose (June 21, 1998). The event was a big success; however, the most memorable moments were Chiling Wu's piano performance, and the little girl May, CK Lee's daughter, dancing to his singing.

With Peter and Sheau-Yin in charge, kitchen was a fun place for volunteers. (1998)

**Our Iron Chefs John and Frank, together with Peter and Sheau-Yin. (1998)**

**Linmei organized the first family hiking trip in summer of 1998.**

**Recognizing our key volunteers at FCSN 2nd Annual Meeting & Family Day.
(June 1999)**

**Recognizing our key volunteers at FCSN 2nd Annual Meeting and Family Day. (1999)**

# PRESIDENT'S MESSAGE 1999

## Tsai-Wei Wu (FCSN President 1999-2000), 2000

**FCSN began to provide more outdoor activities for our member families, such as this family camping at Uvas Canyon County Park in summer 1999.**

On behalf of the FCSN (Friend of Children with Special Needs) board and staff members, I would like to welcome our fresh and senior FCSN members to migrate into the 21st century and continue building a better future for our children.

FCSN has slated its mission "to help individuals with special needs and their families find love, hope, respect, and support through integrated community involvement" since its birth. In the past years, with the leadership of our former president Linmei Chiao and the efforts of all the colleagues, internally, FCSN organization infrastructure has become stronger; and externally, FCSN has earned recognition and praise because of our uniqueness and services. Although our bylaws clearly state that FCSN is a non-profit and non-political organization; however, it does not mean FCSN is self-contained and detached from the outside world. On the contrary, we are very much relying on community resources to help achieve our goals.

Since 1996, FCSN has been fortunately receiving many supports from our community: For example, because of our board member Su-Ti Lin's connection, the Asian Pacific Family Resources Center (APFRC) of Santa Clara County has granted FCSN the use of their facility for our biweekly family gathering event without any charge. In mid-August of this year, the director of APFRC, Ms. Celia Anderson, explicitly said to me that supporting the organizations like FCSN is their essential work. The other example is the County Resources for Families and Communities (RFC) has generously funded FCSN in the past two years. In the private sector, FCSN has also received many financial supports from companies, agencies, and individuals as well.

It goes without saying, community supports do not come by without good reasons. FCSN has earned the support because of our continued efforts, solid results, and hard-earned reputation. All the FCSN credibility is accumulated little by little, day by day from each of you. No operation can be sustained well simply by luck. Therefore, at the beginning of this new school year, I would like to encourage our volunteers and staff members to do the following: In the coming year, please document the work either by yourself or your team, the work such as the project planning, execution and evaluation, etc., those records will be the best testimony to substantiate FCSN's contributions to the community; and in return, those records will also be the best tokens to earn the community support.

In the previous board meeting, I had proposed how to cultivate our FCSN center to becoming a Resources center, Education center, and Comforting center by implementing a set of properly designed activities: To be ready as a Resources center, FCSN has significantly invested in the IT infrastructure in recent years. FCSN has created its own official website and started using emails to improve our com-munication effectiveness. FCSN has issued quarterly newsletter to broadcast the organization news, event schedule, and activity highlights to our members on a regular basis. The first edition of FCSN Family Handbook was released last year, and currently the editing team is working on the second edition. Our small but cozy library has a significant collection of books about development disability and related topics. Our volunteers have compiled and categorized all the video tapes recorded from the past organizational activities, such as the special topic seminars or workshops. Those books and tapes are available to our members whenever they may have the needs.

To be ready as an educational center, we have been using our biweekly Family Regular Gathering event to promote educational and learning activities. For example, we have frequently invited experts/professionals in the field of special education, medical research, finance, or public offices to offer our parents learning opportunities to various subjects, such as, the medical advances in autism and relevant areas, the resources which the county office or school district can provide, our legal rights, and financial planning, etc. The topic coverage is comprehensive, parents-motivated, and very practical.

Regarding of the schooler education aspect, the "activity/involvement" is the key ingredient in all our activities. Under this framework, a teacher not only creates a least restrictive environment for the kids with special needs, but also encourages regular teenager's involvement in an activity. This mechanism allows the participating teenagers to know his or her partners with special needs better via direct interactions throughout the event. As a result, the teenage helper gets chances to observe more behavior details about the partner, so that he or she can understand some issues which might be overlooked or misunderstood by the general public.

We hope, with more teenager's involvement, the young generation would get a better impression to people with special needs. And years later, when the young generation becomes the main pillar of our community, their understanding and personal experience would have tremendous impact to their surroundings, and that impact could change the society's view towards the special needs community. I believe this seeds-spreading work will help steer the community to be more socially involved and create more opportunities for our kids in the future.

The reason why the special education is differentiated from the traditional education system is because it needs a different set of curriculum and teaching skills. Undoubtedly, the compassion and patience are still the commonality between the two education systems and in fact the former system requires far more than the latter. Currently only a small portion of FCSN teachers is with a special education background or related expertise, most of them are teachers from local Chinese schools. Nevertheless, with tremendous passion and love, our teachers are working wonders on our kids; and because of them, FCSN education system has grown quickly and steadily.

I believe that the families with special needs children could have and should have fun and happiness in their life. To achieve this goal, the first step or our top priority is to help those parents in constructing a correct mindset and staying positive in front of their kids, then coach those families to walk away from their misery spirals and guide them onto the right tracks.

The most valuable resource within FCSN is a group of talented parents who have already stepped out of deep trenches, learned how to look at the brighter side and face their challenges positively. Throughout the years, they have successfully changed the atmosphere around them. Behind every one of those parents, there is always a touching story to be told, a story comprises of tears, struggles and courage. Just imagine that a collection of tens of those families' unique journeys in growing up with their loved ones, how abundant and powerful that knowledge could be. By simply sharing those real stories, life experiences, and survival skills with the younger families with special needs, a meaningful and noble mission could be accomplished.

Traditionally, FCSN hosts quite a few large-scale annual events such as the Chinese New Year Celebration Party, Family Camping, Picnic in the Park/Sports Day, and Annual Meeting/Family Day, plus some small-scale events such as the Mother's Day Appreciation Dinner, Thanksgiving potluck, and Christmas Talent Show, etc. The purpose is to not only to provide our stressed parents a moment of relaxation and enjoyment, but also offer our kids a stage to present themselves and have fun. I would like to remind our members, the best reward to our hardworking volunteers and staff is your earnest participation, and the best praise to our kids with special needs is your generous applause.

At the beginning of a new century, let's hold hands and stride forward for our young generation.

**Our biweekly family gathering was not enough to meet the needs of all special needs families. Anna recognized it and organized the first play group in Fremont to serve the specific need of a local group. (1999)**

**Sufen also organized the Almaden Playgroup in 1999.**

**FCSN set up an "information and fun games" booth in RFC's multi-culture family fair, which marks the first time that FCSN participated in a community event. (1999)**

# FROM PRESIDENT'S DESK

## Li-Huei Wei (FCSN President 2000-2001), 2000

**Watching performances at Chinese New Year celebration at APFRC in San Jose. (2000)**

On behalf of the Board of Directors and staff members, I would like to welcome you to FCSN. As we continue our commitment to help children with special needs and their families find hope, love, respect, and support, we hope that you will continue to be with us. Let us envision this new millennium that will be full of excitement and joy for the FCSN family.

FCSN is a group of caring people who commit to help children with special needs. And, as one of many FCSN unique characteristics, one third of our member families are without children with special needs, they are just normal families but with warm hearts and full of love to the society. We all come together to volunteer our time and efforts, at the same time, we also enjoy the resources that other people have contributed.

Thanks to our former chairpersons, Linmei and Tsai-Wei, who had established a solid foundation for FCSN, it is evident that our organization has become stronger and much better positioned in pursuing our slated goals. Thanks to Su-Ti who had guided us to find the Asian Pacific Family Resources Center as the home base for FCSN regular gatherings. Many thanks go to Mrs. Celia Anderson and her wonderful staff at APFRC for not only providing us the excellent facility but also supporting us with childcare service. I am proud that FCSN is being recognized as a model organization in the community and we do play an important role for the families that have children with special needs.

As we are approaching our fourth year, we are so proud of FCSN's Dream Committee. The Dream committee is working on a long-term project that will be beneficial to all the children with special needs. They are planning to build an activity center that can foster job opportunities and leisure activities in the near future. Furthermore, we are also reaching to every member to build mutual support and care, in order to build a warm and lovely community. I am proud to announce that FCSN has expanded its original support group into 4-subgroups: they are the volunteers with children with special needs, volunteers without children with special needs, volunteers with Cantonese-speaking, and volunteers of youth. I would like to encourage you to join one of these support groups and be ready to establish better relationships among members.

Because FCSN is a non-profit organization, your financial support is critically important. Your kind donation would enable us to better serve the needy families. I sincerely thank those individuals and organizations that have been generous to FCSN in the past. We are currently seeking possible community resources for the organization. Your generosity is genuinely welcome and very much appreciated.

Thank you and may God bless you and your family!

**We held a FCSN logo contest, and here (left) is the winning design by Victor Yeh. Subsequently, this design was adopted to become our official logo. (2000)**

# HOW FCSN GOT ITS NAME

## James Chiao (FCSN Co-founder), June 2016

A planning committee was formed in April 1996, and we took turns and met at each other's homes. Front row from the left: Joyce Yeh, Linmei Chiao, Shiow-Luan Chen. Back row from the left: Jim Chiao, Sheau-Yin Hsia, Peter Hsia, Jessie Ho, Lanny Tsai, Teresa Chou, Amy Wang, Jason Wang. (April 27, 1996) The group soon got stronger when Sufen Yeh, Anna Wang, and Jennifer Li joined the committee.

FCSN started with a seminal meeting on April 6th, 1996, at my home in Saratoga. The idea of forming a support group came from Shiow who was the young, energetic special ed teacher who connected with fifteen to twenty Chinese special needs families in the mid-90s. To get more help, my wife, Linmei, also enlisted a few of her best friends to join. At the very first formal meeting, Shiow gave the group a temporary name "South Bay Chinese Family Support Group." At the time, the name made a lot of sense: we were a group of Chinese families, mostly in the South Bay, and a support group was what we wanted.

A planning committee was formed as a result of the seminal meeting, with the goal to form a support group organization. In the second planning meeting on 4/27/96, we spent an hour on naming the group; however, we could not reach a consensus. For weeks, we did not resolve this issue since there was a more fundamental question: whether we should just form a subgroup under an established non-profit organization such as Parents Helping Parents or Association for Chinese Families of the Disabled in San Francisco. At the May 16 meeting, Peter Hsia went through the pros and cons and told us: "It would take lots of time and effort to form a new organization." Yet, we wanted to chart our own course, and decided against forming a subgroup under another organization because we wanted to preserve our culture, values, and retain the freedom to reach our goals.

With the decision to form our own organization, we again found it necessary to decide on a name. In the 6/8/1996 meeting, we voted based on a list of proposals. The result was not surprising: the temporary name "South Bay Chinese Family Support Group" was formally adopted. However, after the meeting, I was not very satisfied with the name. For one, it limited us to a geographic area "South Bay." Secondly, by specifying Chinese, we were limiting ourselves to an ethnic group and a smaller population. At the time, the planning committee was busy with many new projects, such as the babysitting network, integrated classes, library, and summer picnic, with the most important tasks assigned to the ladies. My key assignment was to draft the bylaws – which was not critical to the operation. For months, I worked on the bylaws in my spare time and kept looking for a name that would be more meaningful and more inclusive.

Toward the end of summer, FCSN was getting close to filing papers to apply for Articles of Incorporation and a Federal Tax ID, and whatever name we used would be final. The window to make a name change was closing on us – and we still didn't have a better alternative.

One day, Linmei and I visited our local Saratoga Library which was a place we had visited many times before. On this particular day, as we were leaving the library, my eyes were caught by a plaque hanging near the front entrance. It read, "This library. . .by Friends of Saratoga Library."

Suddenly, a light went on in my head. I asked myself: "If a library can have friends, why not children with special needs?" To me, the word "Friends" so clearly described how our friends had helped us since day one, and how we wanted a community that is more inclusive. Exiting from the library door, I was very excited and told Linmei that we might have the right name: "Friends of Children with Special Needs."

At the 9/14/1996 planning committee meeting, my motion to change the name was put to a vote. Overwhelmingly, the new name was approved. By the end of 1996, our organization was registered as "Friends of Children with Special Needs." That's how our organization finally got its name.

# CHAPTER 2:
# The Dream Project
## *(2001-2006)*

After three years, in 1999, FCSN membership had grown to roughly 200 families. We held bi-weekly family gatherings at Asian Pacific Family Resource Center in San Jose. At one of the board meetings, Linmei proposed the building of a community center as our long-term goal. However, there were lots of doubts since FCSN had no income nor any saving at the time; it was thought that the proposal was an unrealizable dream. Fortunately, the board approved the formation of a "Dream Committee", and appointed Albert Wang, Linmei Chiao, and Peter Hsia to study the proposal.

With the purchase of a vacant land by FCSN parents on Peralta Blvd in Fremont, the proposal took on life and became known as the Dream Project. During the Dream Project years, Albert was FCSN's president for three years in 2001, 2002, and 2005; and Limin Hu and Anna Wang filled the role in 2003 and 2004. Under Albert's leadership, the project team hired an architect and applied for re-zoning to sub-divide the land and build a center on the land donated by PDLLC families. The project gave real hope and meaning to many member families, and the families started raising fund for its construction. In 2002, Albert started fundraising in earnest and volunteered Limin Hu as the chair of our first fundraising gala which was a huge success. Later, Limin went on to produce several wildly successful Chinese folk song concerts with the help of FCSN Fathers Choir. These events generated a lot of interest in the Bay Area Chinese community and raised the awareness of the special needs community and the Dream Project.

The construction of the Dream Center began in 2003. With the success of our fundraising activities and the diligence of our construction team members (Albert Wang, Linmei Chiao, Stanley Woo, and Larry Peng,) architects (Rick Williams and later Sy-Cheng Tsai,) and contractor ACON, the Dream Center construction was completed in summer 2006.

# DREAM PROJECT

## Linmei Chiao (Co-Founder), June 2001

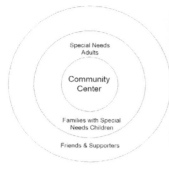

**A group of FCSN parents formed Peralta Dream LLC (PDLLC) to acquire a vacant land in Fremont, part of the land was donated to FCSN to build the Dream Center. (2000)**

Sometimes, the most common person in the world can be involved in a most unique and meaningful endeavor, this is the feeling of my involvement in FCSN's Dream Project.

I have long worried about the future living situation of my special needs son Brian: he could live with us, but we would not be there for him someday. My daughter Tracy is very capable and loving, and she might be able to take care of her brother in the future. But Tracy will have a career, family, and her own world. It would be unfair to burden her with that responsibility.

### Nothing Is Readily Available

Even though Brian is only sixteen years old, I started years ago looking for alternatives in preparation for rainy days; so, what are the options after public education at the age of twenty-two? Thanks to many friends, especially Ling Ru who also has been busy exploring because of her own daughter. I collected information from various organizations, attended many seminars, visited different living arrangements, and talked to many parents, the conclusion I reached was the following: if we take something that is readily available on the market, it might not meet our needs. If we don't work hard now to start something good and set up a new system, there might be more worrying and troubles for us with our children later.

## Our Dream

My wish is that Brian and other special needs adults can live in a clean and comfortable home, away from parents; they live in harmony with others and in a safe community. Their potential and strength can be recognized, they can feel safe, confident, comfortable, and happy. How can we reach this ideal situation?

The parents and guardians of special needs adults are the ones who understand their needs best. Therefore, we envision that we will have parents-organized support group to help with their children's programs, and to actively participate in the design and improvement of the program content and schedule. With proper support and management, parents and volunteers can freely make suggestions, work closely with FCSN, and help each other's kids. Our special needs adult children will be so blessed living in this community, the parents could form a close-knit group, and volunteers' work would become more meaningful!

In recent years, laws have been passed to require special needs individuals to be in the least restrictive environment and be integrated into the mainstream communities. However, to be totally integrated into a community is exceedingly difficult in practice. Therefore, the Dream Project plans to combine a bit of the old-fashioned group home concept with the new supported living idea, to create a community-like environment for the Supported Living arrangement.

Just as normal supported living, our supported living apartment will look like a normal apartment. Special needs individuals will live with their roommates and caregivers in the apartment, and the Supported Living service will cover the cost of the caregivers. What is different from the standard supported living model is that we will put a few of these apartments together in the same community, so it would be easier to manage. The management and operation could be more centralized and efficient, and with many friends in the same community, the apartment becomes a safer and happier place.

For higher function independent living special needs adults, they typically receive a limited number of visits from social workers, which often means not quite enough care or support. In the Dream Project, we may mix them together with those in Supported Living service who require more support. The higher function clients can be trained to help those who typically need more support. In this fashion, the caregiver's workload might be reduced, and those in independent living could receive more support they need and be proud to help others.

Supported Living apartment will be close to the proposed Fremont Center, which could provide day programs, job training, social, recreational, and volunteering opportunities. Management team in Fremont Center also can train and support the staff working in the apartment. Since FCSN's founding, we have always rented space for our activities, with severe limitations on its time and frequency. For the long term, it is best to have our own facility. With our own Center, we'll need a regular income to sustain its operation. By running Adult Day Program and job training programs, we can generate some income to pay for the staff and the maintenance of the Center. With the supported living apartments nearby, FCSN Center can have a supply of clients and users.

## Dream Project Status

Dream Project started from nothing but an idea, in June 2000, a group of FCSN families formed Peralta Dream LLC, and with the help from Albert Wang, they purchased a 1.5-acre lot in Fremont. Now it is being designed by an architect, so we can apply for rezoning in the Fremont planning department. The initial concept is to divide the lot into two parcels, one half would be used to build supported living housing, and the other half would be donated to FCSN and be used to build FCSN Center. If everything goes according to plan, we can start the pre-sale of the apartments in two years. With donations from parents from part of the fund in selling the apartments and money from various fundraising activities, we should be able to complete the construction of the Center. This year, the design team and architects have faced many challenges such as: how do we get approval from the city planning department and gain support from our neighbors? How to reduce the cost of the construction? How do we come up with a design that meets our needs and looks good?

While we are witnessing the realization of our dream, we still have a long way to go, and need the support and encouragement of our members. On the other hand, our hearts are filled with gratitude and warmth. We want to thank all the participating volunteers, donors, and all who care and supported us. God's willing, our dreamland will appear in front of us very soon.

**With performers dancing to the Beatles' tune "*Yellow Submarine*", cheerleaders, a food booth, and many volunteers, FCSN had a strong presence at a summer fair in Cupertino Park. (2001)**

**We first celebrated Mother's Day in 1997, and it has become a very popular event. Here, we are celebrating Mother's Day at APFRC in San Jose in May 2001.**

**TCAAT is a sporting events for Bay Area Chinese & Taiwanese Community, and it seems like an event not suited for people with special needs. Not to be left out, we held our own special games as part of TCAAT in Cupertino. (2001)**

# PRESIDENT'S REMARK 2002

## Albert Wang (President 2001-2002), June 2002

Time really flies. Another school year is about to end. I would like to express my sincere appreciation for all of you who made this year another success. Our enrollment has increased, more volunteers want to participate in our programs, our outreach effort is paying off with more and more families calling to inquire about our program and seeking help, and our dream, the FCSN Center, is on the verge of approval by the City of Fremont

First, I would like to congratulate seven of our members who were recognized by the local Chinese American organizations as Model Mom's on May 11, 2002. Chi-Ling Wu's piano performance and the FCSN ("Fathers" of Children with Special Needs) singing group won wide praises from the audience of 300+ people during the recognition party. In reality, all of our member mothers deserve such honor. Families of special needs children cannot continue without the

44

dedication and sacrifice of the mothers. Congratulations to Linmei Chiao, Anna Wang, Lihuei Wei, Linda Yang, Hsiou-Lian Kun, Iris Chien and Su-Fen Wu, and salute to all of the mothers in our group.

Thanks to the interest and effort of Ms. Jo Wan of Channel 26, KTSF News, FCSN and its Dream Project was featured for 5 consecutive days during both the Cantonese and Mandarin news programs. We have received dozens of calls from families seeking information, interested donors and volunteers, as well as other groups of similar nature making the connection for future collaboration. Ms. Wan's series will go a long way in helping FCSN achieve its mission of serving more children with special needs and building our permanent home.

Over the past three weeks, there appears to be significant confusion about the relationship between FCSN and the newly formed Organization of Special Needs Families (OSF). I believe it's important to explain this issue clearly to our membership. OSF is formed by former FCSN Board member Lihuei Wei and meets in Cupertino. It is an organization independent of FCSN, with no financial or operational ties. It is not a branch of FCSN in Cupertino.

FCSN operates bi-weekly programs at the Asian Pacific Family Resources Center, the Milpitas and the Almaden playgroups. When our dream project is completed, we will also operate day and evening/weekend programs in our Fremont center, while maintaining APFRC and other local groups to meet our members' needs.

It has been a great pleasure to serve as your President for the last year. I have learned a great deal from all of our family members and dedicated volunteers. I look forward to meeting more of you in the future. Let's all work together to improve the lives of our children with special needs.

# FCSN'S FIRST FUNDRAISING GALA, AND MY FIRST TOO

## Limin Hu (Gala chair), Dec 2002

**Singer Ka-Wai Ho from Canada provided a special star appearance (left). A skit was performed by Hua Yi Performing Art Group (upper right) and the music was accompanied by CMEA Band (lower right).**

## Getting Hooked

I still remember attending this Big Event meeting at the end of May. FCSN's President Albert Wang, M.D. invited an array of talents and active community leaders to plan for a major fundraising event. After the meeting, I was very impressed with so many great ideas this group came up to raise money through a fundraising gala.

The next thing I knew was that Albert asked me to be the event chair. Without any experience with this kind of event, not even knowing the terms that everyone was talking intimately – backdrop, MC, truss lights, etc., in addition to not knowing people well enough within FCSN, I was crazy enough to take on the co-chair role to assist Albert on this major undertaking. I believed in the Dream Project and Albert's grand vision, but a major fundraising gala of this scale at Hyatt Regency did seem like a daunting task. Therefore, we adopted the theme "Impossible Dream" for the event initially.

"The fundraising gala to raise $100,000 is impossible, but we have to do it." I felt strongly that we do need to educate and market to the Chinese American communities in order to make our dream come true.

My role was supposed to be an assistant to Albert on the dream event, but he quietly dropped his co-chair role one day quoting prior commitments and the fact that I bought his previous house. This is how I became hooked as the event chair.

## Getting Started

In the beginning, our progress was slow since we were just struggling to figure out how to get outside talents to assist this event, how to push for media coverage, how to get internal FCSN staff to help on things they don't have experience, and how to unite the entire FCSN to support this event.

There are many friends who came to my rescue. I always remembered Herb Chiu joining Albert to provide advice to me almost on a daily basis; the kind and quick responses from Macy Mak and Joyce Chang to work side by side with me; Linmei and Sufen taking on the responsibility of FCSN children's performance; Jim Chiao's faithful devotion from the beginning to the end; Joyce Hu's excellent work on invitation package and artwork; and Anna and Linda's dedication. With so many friends behind me, we changed the theme to "Make Our Dreams Come True." We prepared the invitation brochure and sponsor solicitation package, and arranged the pre-sale of raffle tickets at the end of July. Now the fun part starts....

## Relentlessly Going After Alumni and Associations

Dinner tickets with a price tag of $75 were not exactly an easy sell in today's economy. In order to get 800 guests, we needed an aggressive sales campaign to the Chinese American communities. We were pulling every string and taking every opportunity to distribute our gala invitation.

We first started it with a Lake Tahoe camping trip hosted by the Joint Alumni Association of Chinese Universities and Colleges in Northern California during Labor Day's weekend to promote our Dream Event. Together with kids, Anna, Linda, Nai-Ping, Christine and I put on quite a show for the joint alumni. It was an unforgettable show that we led the crowd for chicken dances in the dark fluorescent light, wearing all black shirts with white gloves and white waistbands.

Our effort to spread the news to as many associations as possible finally paid off when our name FCSN and our Dream Project became famous among local communities later on.

## First Taste with Media

In August, I had sent many emails, called many media friends that others referred to me, and sent press releases to the media, with no avail. Through Albert and Joyce's great relationship with the media, we started to build a relationship with them in September. Albert also started to engage in a large-scale email campaign to plead for support from everyone while we were at Lake Tahoe camping.

The first press coverage related to the event was on Sing Tao Daily, and the reporter mistakenly advertised for the support for Peralta Apartment, instead of the Dream Event and Center. Then

Anna, Joyce and I went to the first Sing Tao Chinese Radio interview, and it was in Cantonese! Thank God that both Anna and Joyce speak Cantonese. Otherwise, you could imagine my response when the host Ivy asked me "Limin, what do you have to add to Anna and Joyce's comments?" while I had no clue about their Cantonese conversation.

The breakthrough with the media finally happened in the second half of September, when we had our first press conference at Natori restaurant on September 20. Also, my company Ellie Mae, Inc. got a major award from San Francisco Business Times for the fastest growing private company in the Bay Area. Media started to know me better, and we finally convinced the media that the Dream Project is a worthy and noble effort. Suddenly the media coverage started to snowball, and I had been on newspapers and radios for more than a dozen of times. However, the gala is only a month away, and we still had very few people responded to our invitation.

Eventually we garnered the support from Channel 26 KTSF, World Journal, Sing Tao Daily, Sing Tao Chinese Radio, San Jose Mercury News, San Francisco Business Times, Sina.com and SanFranciscoChinatown.com. We had accomplished one of the two major missions for the Dream Event Gala – spreading the seeds to everyone. Now we just needed to sell tickets and raise $100,000 for our FCSN Center.

## Program Book

Even though Albert and I put into overdrive and spared no effort for the dream event, but we both were so busy besides the dream event. There were plenty of fires to be put out at Ellie Mae, Inc. that I started to work so late. I still remembered exchanging emails with Albert sometimes deep into night like 2 or 3 AM in the morning. I didn't know how he did it, but I often took brief naps whenever I got an opportunity during the day. However, Anna and Christine were relentless in the pursuit of greatness for the dream event. They talked to the press, solicited sponsors, sold raffle tickets, updated website, created program for ticket control, and the list goes on and on.

Again, we proved the power of FCSN's teamwork and dedication. Together, we established twenty-seven pages of sponsorships and ads. Christine single-handedly took on the program book, not because she chose to do so. She dropped everything else and worked on it for two straight weeks sleeping only four hours every day. I found her sleeping on the couch every morning. Our beautiful 48-page program book turned out to be one of the greatest accomplishments with plenty of praises. My salute to Anna and Christine as they were the unsung heroines behind the scenes.

## Ticket Sale

Program book is one of the most time-consuming tasks, but the ticket sale is the most critical one. The story for ticket sales was similar to the media coverage and program book stories that we were seriously short on the attendance in the beginning. We had already committed 450 seats to the hotel, and it would be a major embarrassment if we fell short, not to mention the loss of money. Despite all our efforts reaching out to Chinese American communities and the broad media coverage, the response from the public remained limited to only a few tables. We realized that the key to success was really hinged on FCSN's internal support.

During the board meeting on Saturday October 5, we broke the news that Jay Stone Shih had accepted our invitation to be the master of ceremony, and we pleaded for support from all board members and staff. Somehow, I could see the sparkles from the eyes of all board members and staff, and I knew that the impossible is now possible.

FCSN is such a wonderful family that we'll make anything possible. This reminded me of a motto that I learned in the past: TEAM means Together Everyone Achieves More. The board members and staff had recruited astonishing 38 tables of guests to the gala!

The last two weeks before the dream event can only be described as hectic. John Yang was working around the clock on the backdrop decoration, and everyone came to my house to help with the event preparation. I probably should ask FCSN to reimburse some of my electricity bills since the lights stayed on usually until 3AM every day. Anna came to my house to work so often and so late that Albert thought she might have moved back to their old house. (For people who don't know, I bought Albert's house last summer.)

The number of guests was 470 two weeks ago before October 26, and then the number jumped to 570, 650, 750, 850, and eventually reached 930. It was a miracle, and we were so happy that we needed to work so hard to accommodate the crowd! Just imagine the table decoration crew from ACFD that Joyce Chang was leading, they had to go out again and again to get material and worked overtime for the additional tables.

## Dream Event Day

The event was unforgettable with 93 tables and more than 1,000 people including guests, performers, and volunteers. There are plenty of items to improve like the sound and stage setup, and program control, but our children's performance and parent sharing have touched the audience so much that we received a very thick stack of checks just on that day. WE DID IT!

## Closing Remarks

After the accounting closed for the event, we have raised more than $170,000 after deduction of all costs. There are still checks coming in as a result of the dream event. As I was writing this article, Albert informed me of a $10,000 check coming from a touched dream event guest. HURRAY!

Albert has planned many events in the past, and he indicated that "For a first-time event by a Chinese American organization, this was unprecedented in its scope, attendance, and fund raised. It is a validation of FCSN's mission and the widespread community support for our group." In addition to the fund raised, FCSN reached out to thousands of families who may need its services, as well as potential volunteers and donors who will be needed as FCSN expands our service areas and program variety.

This event would not be successful without the support of all of our members, the Association of Chinese Families of the Disabled, and many, many kind-hearted community leaders. It was my great pleasure to work with so many dedicated individuals who put in countless hours of hard work to make it happen, and I just want to say THANK YOU ALL again.

**Two Bay Area celebrities: KTFS 26 TV show "Crosstalk" host, Jay Sone Shih, served as the Master of Ceremony (left), and Mr. Sunny Liu (right) delivered an innovative speech to encourage all the audiences.**

# PRESIDENT'S MESSAGE 2002

## Albert Wang (President 2002), Dec. 2002

**FCSN's fundraising gala "Make Our Dream Come True". (2002)**

Most of you have heard about our extremely successful "Make Our Dreams Come True" gala dinner on 10/26/02, attended by nearly 1000 guests and raised $180,000 net. It is an extraordinary effort by our Event Chair Limin Hu and numerous volunteers and donors. It is heart-warming to know that so many people care.

Along with the successful fundraiser and all the publicity that went with it comes many calls for help from needy families. Due to various limitations, we're not able to accommodate everyone who wishes to join us. This is something very difficult for me. As an organization, FCSN should be able to help everyone coming to us with needs.

The space shortage can partly be addressed when our center is built. But a shortage of consistent and experienced volunteers also placed restrictions on our ability to provide services. FCSN believes that working side-by-side toward the same goal will bring us closer together. If you're a new(er) family, we ask that you help us in any way you can, be it in security, setting up/cleaning, kitchen, teaching a class, library, local groups. . .The basis of FCSN is the family unit. We can only become the "big family" we strive for if all members contribute their shares.

Please feel free to contact myself or my wife Anna, or our volunteer training coordinator Jason Hwan. Have a great Holiday Season! See you at our Christmas Party or our next semester!

# PRESIDENT'S MESSAGE 2003

## Albert Wang (President), June 2003

**FCSN Board of Directors at Annual Meeting and Family Day. (2003)**

It's amazing how time flies! With the blink of an eye, I'm about to complete my second year as the President of FCSN. Reflecting back on the two years, I'm very proud to say that FCSN has really pulled together as a group and now functions smoothly, moving toward our mission to provide more services for children with special needs and their families.

2002-2003 has seen some tremendous successes at FCSN. We have expanded our services with new programs – two local groups in the Cupertino/Saratoga area, two groups in Fremont, a Cantonese language support group in Oakland, and a very active informal Almaden playgroup. They serve different age ranges and cater to the local need in their format and programs. Our seminars have become so popular that we often have to add seats to accommodate the crowd. The bi-weekly gathering at Asian Pacific Family Resource Center in San

Jose has grown so fast that we had to limit registration to avoid security and safety issues, adding further impetus to the need of our own center. To reach our mission of integrating special needs individuals into the community, we need to take every opportunity to educate the public. To this end, FCSN has greatly expanded our publicity effort. Our organization and members have appeared in major articles of the San Jose Mercury News, Fremont Argus, Channel 7 KGO TV, Channel 26 KTSF, China Crosstalk show by Stone Shih, Chinese Radio, World Journal, Sing Tao Daily, and many other media outlets. Each time someone reads about us, he/she gains a little more insight into the special needs community and removes a layer of apprehension in dealing with our children. Our dream is that, someday, our children will be treated just as a member of the community, not someone "different" or "special".

Despite the severe economic downturn in our area, FCSN nevertheless had a successful year in fundraising. With the generous pledge of the Peralta Dream LLC to donate the site for the FCSN Center, we are now more than halfway to our fundraising goal. Our board, staff, and membership have put together all their resources to get to where we are. We must redouble our effort in the home stretch. With everyone's help, I am confident that we'll be able to break ground for the "Dream Center" once we successfully navigate through the maze of governmental regulations, hopefully sometime this summer or fall. We must pay careful attention to continue to serve more families better.

First is the need for continued improvement in our programs. We have assembled a top-notch team of advisors, in addition to the invaluable expertise within our families developed through life experience. We must apply this knowledge to develop more programs to suit the needs of children of all functioning levels and disabilities who seek our help. We need to establish a system to measure the progress of our children over time so we can fine-tune our programs further.

Secondly, it is important to develop future leadership in our organization. I am a firm believer that a successful group must provide those interested with the opportunity to put forth his/her vision and lead the group to even higher grounds. With changing leadership from time to time, we can gain a wider perspective of our mission and grow in a more balanced direction. Fortunately, FCSN continues to attract many talented families, both with and without special needs children, into our midst. If you have the heart for special needs children, identify with our mission, feel you can contribute, and are willing to work toward our goal, please step forward and take charge of an existing program, propose a new program, serve on the board, or volunteer in the numerous areas where we desperately need support.

FCSN is now at a critical juncture. I believe it is no longer feasible to expect such a large and complex organization to be fully supported by volunteers. We must "professionalize" our organization. The new FCSN Center, when completed, will demand the attention of full-time staff members to fully utilize its space to serve our community. To prepare for this eventuality, and to support the many upcoming events, FCSN has hired its first executive director, Josephine Chou. She comes with a strong background in management and accounting, where our need is the greatest. She has also been our classroom volunteer for more than a year now, showing her true love for our children. I hope all of you will take a moment to welcome her aboard and introduce yourselves to her.

It was a humbling experience to serve as your President for the last two years. While it required many long meetings and late-night sessions to meet task deadlines, it was an unforgettable experience for me. I have learned so much from working with many of you and facing often-unexpected challenges. I will always treasure the many friends I've made here. And I will continue to support FCSN in its next phase of critical growth.

**Recognizing volunteers of the year at our Annual Meeting and Family Day. (2003)**

We usually held our family gathering indoor at APFRC in San Jose on Saturdays. On this particular Saturday, for some reason, we were locked out of the APFRC facility. Instead, this memorable family gathering was held outdoor at Kelly Park; it was a lot of fun as the session turned into a family picnic that was highlighted by a beauty contest and a singing performance by Father's Choir. (2003)

# OUR DREAM WILL COME TRUE

## Limin Hu (President), 2003

### *Dream Center Groundbreaking on Oct. 22, 2003*

**FCSN held a groundbreaking ceremony for its Dream Center on Oct. 22, 2003 at Peralta Blvd in Fremont.**

I feel very fortunate to be the President of this great family. FCSN is now widely recognized by the Chinese American community as one of the best nonprofit charity organizations in the bay area. As a result, FCSN has many loyal members, dedicated board and staff, and a huge base of supportive volunteers and followers. This is a great validation of FCSN's effort in serving the special needs community. I'm proud to be a "FCSNer"! Thank you everybody for your selfless effort and great teamwork!

At the same time, I also feel the great responsibilities that the board has placed on my shoulders. FCSN is now transitioning from a family-based organization to a well-structured charity, and there are many great challenges at this juncture. The first thing that I have focused on in my presidency is to revise the FCSN bylaws to reflect the need to enhance the rules that govern the structure and operation of this great organization. The second priority for me is to make sure we have an open book and clean financial records with yearly financial audits that we can ensure that all donation dollars and volunteer effort are put to the best use for our mission.

Beyond those two priorities, the biggest challenge for me is the Dream Project. Before I go into the details, I'd like to take this opportunity to express my gratitude to our ex-President Albert Wang, M.D. Albert's vision and drive had turned the impossible dream into a possibility. We have raised $1.5 million in just over a year's time frame, and we are now only half a million dollars short of our $2 million goal to construct and equip our Dream Center. Let's work together and push ahead with 110% of our effort and OUR DREAM WILL COME TRUE! Also, we should be very proud that this center will be the first ever project of its kind in the state, and possibly in the whole country!

**First Chinese folk song concert, organized by Limin Hu, was held at Santa Clara Convention Center theatre. This event generated a lot of interest in the Bay Area Chinese community and raised the awareness of the special needs community and the Dream Project. (2003)**

**Performers & organizers took the final stage at the 2nd Chinese Campus Folk Song Concert in 2004.**

# LAYING THE FOUNDATION FOR OUR DREAM COMMUNITY

## Anna Wang (President), Dec. 2004

**CDPPAT "My Dream" performance inspired the audience by the achievement and moving performance of these special needs artists.**

I am extremely blessed to be the President of our FCSN family. I feel like a mother for all our beloved children. In the past year, under Limin's leadership, FCSN has made tremendous strides in bringing much-needed programs to many localities, building great community support, and fundraising for our Dream Center. It's a tough act to follow. My focus for this year is to strengthen our bonds through support and friendship for our enormous organization, bringing back the sense of love of a close-knit family. To help me achieve this goal, we are fortunate to have a "Dream Team" as our executive committee. We have two vice presidents. One of them is Shiow, our founder and special education consultant. Even though she doesn't have any special needs children of her own, her passion for all special needs children is unsurpassed by anyone. She often called herself a "fan" for our children. Our second vice president is Yee-Yeen. His dedication, communication and organization skills are true assets to our team. Fundraising, accounting, and keeping a close tab on the center building progress are definitely not my strength. But, with the help of Nhon, our secretary and fundraising chair, Amy, our treasurer, and Limin, our Board Advisor, my mind can be at ease with these awesome responsibilities. Together, with our dedicated Board and staff members, we will strive to fulfill our mission of bringing 'love, hope, and respect to our special needs children and their families through integrated community involvement'.

In the past few months, I've been touched by the outpouring of encouragement, and support from our community. We had three very successful fundraising events, bringing us within just $100K short of our fundraising goal of $2 million. The first of these was "The Dream" by the Chinese Disabled People Performing Arts Troupe. Our children, our families, and the entire audience were inspired by the achievement and moving performance of these special needs artists. I would like to take this opportunity to thank the "Dream Production" team of Gayle Chan, Michael Chan, and Macy Mak Chan. They were instrumental in putting the shows together and soliciting all the sponsors for the event. We then made history with our Folksong Concert in July. Over 4000 people packed the two concerts at the Flint Center. Everyone enjoyed the wonderful music that brought back sweet memories of college years. The beautiful performance of our children brought tears to the eyes of many. And at the end of October, we had another successful Gala. All these events were humongous undertakings. Many of our members, volunteers, and supporters put in countless hours to ensure our success. They are the real heroes behind the scenes. It's impossible to list all of them and I am afraid to miss a few. We would really like to express to all of them our deepest APPRECIATION for their effort and contribution to our FCSN family. We have shown the world what unity and love can do for the community.

In the summer, we had many fun and nourishing activities. Besides our usual July 4th Parade, Sports Day, Athletic Tournament, and camping, we also had our first Annual Parents Workshop, and Bowling Tournament. Yes, we had a busy, joyful time together. But, like any other family, FCSN has its share of tears. In May, one of our precious children, Brandon Chen, passed away due to a sudden illness. Gracie and Jia (Brandon's parents) were overcome with grief and shock. We felt a tremendous loss at FCSN. Many of us attended the funeral and grieved with the family. We were also deeply impressed by Gracie's company, Aradigm, which raised a memorial fund "In Memory of Brandon" for our future center. We will never forget his angelic smile and trust that he is in God's loving arms. On October 20, Brandon's baby brother, Vincent arrived, bringing much happiness to Gracie, Jia, and all of us.

If it takes a village to raise a child, we certainly need the entire community to pull together to raise our children with special needs. It's our goal to bring our 400 family members together into a big family to support each other and to love each other. As we close the gap of our fundraising goal for our Dream Center, we need your help to bring closeness to our community and strengthen our bonds. A House is not a Home until we Furnish it with Love. Please attend our many family programs and activities, be a mentor parent or volunteer. Let's join hands to build our loving community and a brighter future for the special needs children and the families.

HAPPY HOLIDAYS!!!

**FCSN Center under construction. (2004)**

# HISTORY IN THE MAKING

## Anna Wang (President 2004), June 2005

### *Building a Dream Community for our Special Children*

**FCSN joined the Capitol Action Day Rally to protest the state budget cut and fight for the disability rights.**

It is with great humbleness that I write this message. FCSN has the most wonderful group of volunteers who make our mission possible. I want to thank all those who put in their time, effort, financial resources, and energy to help us "build a community of love, hope and respect for our special needs children".

This year, our Governor again proposed numerous budget cuts to the disability community. Once again, FCSN united the parents to be the VOICE of the VOICELESS. A large group of parents and children went to Sacramento, on May 24, Capitol Action Day, to protest against the budget proposal. FCSN has shown California that the Chinese American Community is active in advocating for our children and fighting for disability rights. The Capitol Action Day organizers were so impressed by our rally last year that they used FCSN's group photo on the cover of their official 2005 Capitol Action Day flyer.

We continue to give tremendous support to our special needs children and their families. We currently offer twenty-five programs in fifteen different locations from Oakland, Fremont, Milpitas, San Jose, Cupertino, Saratoga, Los Gatos, to Palo Alto. For children, we offer playgroups, therapy classes, after-school enrichment program, yoga classes, computer classes and life-skill training. As our children grow older, we further our support to include job training programs. We are proud to begin our first adult-based jobs program with the FCSN booth in Cupertino. To help the parents, we started more parent support gatherings, and the mentor parent program, to build permanent friendship among us. FCSN wants to be the extended family for all our members.

Our center construction has started. I am especially impressed by our center construction team, led by Larry Peng and Stanley Woo, who wake up early every Friday to monitor the construction progress. As of today, the main structure of the center building is in place, and we anticipate occupancy at the end of this year. Parallel to the construction effort is the "software", or program development, of our "Dream Center". We are in search of an executive director with knowledge and experience in establishing and running superior programs for special needs individuals from infancy to adulthood. This will be an excellent opportunity for a self-motivated leader to build an innovative model for others to follow. Our recruitment effort is just starting. Please recommend anyone you know who can fit this profile and lead FCSN to the next level.

The past year has been a great challenge for FCSN as well as for me personally. Our regular family support gathering location had to change again due to the size of the facilities. Our program structure has changed somewhat, requiring creative adjustment by everyone involved. Our Dream Team of dedicated volunteers did the necessary modifications and made our gathering enjoyable for the participants. As for me, I was diagnosed with early-stage cancer in October 2004. After two surgeries, radiation treatment, and "The Chicken Soup" that our FCSN sisters prepared especially for me, I am now as good as new if not better than ever.

As you know, my goal as this year's president is to strengthen the family spirit of our rapidly growing group. Through parent gatherings and mentoring program, as well as our local groups encouraging more participation of the members, we have taken the first step. Now that we are such a huge organization, there's much work to be done if we want to continue making FCSN successful – the family spirit. We have wonderful activities for the whole family in the summer. Please check the summer schedule in the latter part of this newsletter. Let's all connect with at least one family whom we do not know well over the summer months.

I again want to thank our board and staff for their perseverance so we can serve more families with ever more diverse needs. I am so honored to be part of the History in the Making – Building a Dream Community for Our Special Children.

# ADULT DAY PROGRAM

## Linmei Chiao (Program Director), Dec. 2005

### *Becoming a certified vendor of the Regional Center*

**Linmei speaking at FCSN Booth's grand opening in 2004.**

FCSN parents and volunteers have many dreams for our children and adults with special needs. Today, our dream of an FCSN Center is quickly being realized. Another important dream is to make FCSN a certified vendor of the Regional Center. This way, utilizing available governmental funding and resources, FCSN can effectively support and manage various programs that fit the needs of our special needs adults.

In 2004, immediately after the start of construction for the FCSN Fremont Center, a few brave parents and volunteers from South Bay, with very limited experiences and resources, began applying to become an Adult Day Program (ADP) vendor of the San Andreas Regional Center (SARC). They hope to learn the process of running a vendored program by doing so to pave the way for more programs at the coming FCSN Center and the entire Bay Area, to serve more special needs children and adults.

Normally, it takes roughly two months for the application process to go through; however, because of our lack of experience, it took us close to a year. During the long period of waiting, some special needs students chose to attend other programs; and some teachers and volunteers also had other plans. For a period of time, it put a lot more pressure on us because of dwindling support; however, now all of these issues are behind us. FCSN South Bay ADP (Adult Day Program) finally opened in June 2005, with three special needs adults, two part-time teachers, and one volunteer director. Even though we had limited resources, we strived for the best, and we were not skimpy in providing professional diagnostic tests, and teaching materials. In addition, we had to do everything from scratch including many big and small challenges, such as finding a location, moving furniture, getting quality computers, arranging for teacher training... etc.

Luckily, all the hard work eventually paid off. After we opened the program, we got more volunteers, and the program began to move forward. Many parents and social workers, who were sitting on the sideline, began to send special needs individuals our way. Today, our first group has reached its capacity of four individuals, and the second group is ready to start on Jan. 3, 2006. It is most rewarding to see our special needs students learning happily while becoming more confident. Basically, our FCSN South Bay ADP has the following characteristics:

1. It is in a comfortable environment, integrated with the community, with neighbors who willingly provide extra spaces for us to use.

2. We have a few excellent teachers and volunteers to teach and supervise the following classes: drawing, exercise, craft, among others.

3. We opened our own gift shop: FCSN Booth, which provides an ideal place for job training.

4. We have kept the class small to maintain our program's quality.

5. We emphasize the teaching of social skills, communication skills, and proper behavior.

6. We stress the importance of good health, proper diet, and daily exercise.

7. Besides living skills and vocational skills, we also teach practical reading and math.

Every special needs student who attends FCSN South Bay ADP, has a formal ISP (Individualized Service Plan) meeting after three months. I remember on Sept. 13th, after our first ISP meeting, a Chinese American social worker said to us: "I am really proud that the Chinese Americans have such a good program". With encouragement like that, how can we not work even harder?

We still have a long way to go, in early October 2005, FCSN applied to become a vendor for SLS (Adult Supported Living Service) and ILS (Adult Independent Living Service) from RCEB (Regional Center of East Bay). If everything goes according to plan, the application could be approved by the end of 2005. Even though the South Bay Adult Day Program is a small pilot program, it gives us the confidence to move forward. As long as we work together, even without too much experience, the parents and volunteers can create various high quality, unique, and much-needed programs. Let's all work together to realize our dreams!

**Ribbon cutting ceremony at the grand opening of FCSN Booth. (2004)**

# BUILDING A DREAM COMMUNITY

## Albert Wang (President 2005-2006), Dec 2005

It is with great excitement that I'm writing to you, our members, and supporters, about our Dream Center's Progress. Despite some unexpected obstacles and delays, our center in Fremont is scheduled to be completed in January 2006. My recent site visit revealed a beautifully designed building, with welcoming space and sky lights at the entrance, the spacious resource library, classrooms, office, multi-purpose room, and kitchen. It is the product of the cumulative effort of our board, staff, membership, and, most of all, our entire community. You probably don't know that every early Friday morning, rain or shine, for over a year, our volunteer construction management team, headed by Larry Peng and Stanley Woo, meet at the site to be sure every detail is taken care of. You probably don't know the many trips our team members made to the city offices to obtain permits, to the architects to change design, to the hardware store to study fixtures and material, to the flooring store to match color and style . . .

However, the completion of the building does not mean our task is accomplished. To have the building and not the best program within is akin to a computer without software. Our program team, headed by Linmei Chiao and Anna Wang, have also been working hard to be sure we have a quality program to serve our community. I'm happy to report that, with the help of Alameda County Supervisor Scott Haggerty, we have received funding to support our program set up. FCSN has enlisted consultants specializing in this field to help us navigate the maze of governmental regulations so our program will be established to fit our community's needs. This process is well under way, and we hope to have program running when our center fully opens in the Spring of 2006.

There is yet another major task to build a successful organization. We need professional staff to ensure continuity in our program and vision, and coordinate our vast volunteer force to maximize its effectiveness. It is our most critical need at this juncture to have an experienced executive director. If you know of anyone who is willing to take on the exciting challenge of setting direction for our fledgling organization and implement our programs, please contact me or Limin Hu. You can find information about the position on our website www. fcsn1996.org.

It is with the deepest appreciation and the greatest respect to our team that I write these words today. While we reflect upon the successes of FCSN during this joyful season, let's not forget those who are less fortunate than we are. We should reach out and embrace families who need our support. And, only with a united heart and spirit, we can build our dream community. We dream of a world where disabilities are accepted by all. A world where families no longer have to feel ashamed, but rather feel proud to integrate with the rest of society. A world where disabled children and adults alike are not viewed with fear or despise, but accepted with open arms. A world where the disabled, their families, and the community at large come together to care for everyone within.

I recently read a quote from Peter Drucker – "The Best Way to Predict the Future is to Create It Yourself". It really reflects the FCSN spirit well. Let's create our future by joining our hands and working together!!

# FCSN: PAST, PRESENT, AND FUTURE

Albert Wang (President 2005-2006), June 2006

Can't believe it's ten years ago when the initial group of families gathered and decided we should organize. Chinese Americans with disabled children were an obscure group, hidden away from society. The unjustified shame, guilt, depression, anger, denial. . . were too much to bear in our culture of conformity, intolerance, and the lack of understanding and care for the disabled. It was upon this backdrop that Friends of Children with Special Needs was born.

At the beginning, our goal was not grand. We simply wanted a network of families with similar concerns to have a place to share, support each other, exchange information to help our children, and advocate for their basic rights. Some of us with older children wanted to help those whose children were newly diagnosed to bypass the feeling of despair and time wasted researching education opportunities, treatment options, legal rights, social services. . . and go on to a positive life of making the best of the situation, courageously face the world, rid the shame and guilt, and move forward. Others, without special needs children, were kind-hearted individuals who care for our children and want them to be part of society, accepted and loved by all. Therefore, our mission was established – to help children with special needs and their families to find hope, love, respect, and support through integrated community involvement.

Today, ten years later, we have accomplished that and much more. Our program now spans 25 sites, covering playgroups, academics, life skills, job training, seminars, physical fitness, etc. Thanks to our members' willingness to share their experience with the world, and the support of ethnic media and our elected officials, disability is now much more accepted. The key to our success is our core value to empower families to help themselves, not just providing services. We strongly believe this is much more valuable in the long run – teaching families "how to fish" rather than "feed them the fish", so to speak. This is the most important distinction between FCSN and most other organizations serving this population. Our families no longer have to isolate themselves. They can proudly show their children, and be accepted by their neighbors, co-workers, schools, and places of worship. Our advocacy has contributed to protecting the meager benefit from the state government during budget cuts. And our "Dream Center" received unprecedented community support and will be in operation very soon.

Looking forward, I believe we must now transition FCSN into a "system-driven" organization with the launching of our East Bay Adult Day Program, Supported Living and Independent Living Programs, and the soon-to-come extension of current children's programs at the new center, while maintaining and extending our local program in the South Bay. With the help of our Chairman Limin Hu, Executive Director Josephine Chou, Treasurer Anita Ho, we are building an even stronger foundation in anticipation of the opening of our "Dream Center". Please join us, hand in hand, to grow our successful model so more and more families will benefit.

# GRAND OPENING OF FCSN DREAM CENTER

## James Chiao (President 2006-2007), Oct 2006

**Ribbon cutting ceremony during the grand opening of the Fremont Center (Oct. 2006)**

Good afternoon, distinguished guests, ladies and gentlemen, and friends of FCSN:

Thank you all for coming to FCSN Center's grand opening. We have been waiting for this day for a long time. The Center construction started over two years ago, and for a while seems never going to end. Then over a month ago, one morning when I first saw the FCSN sign erected in front of the building, it took my breath away. I realized that this project is coming to an end, and this is finally our home. As many of you know, this center is also called FCSN Dream Center, and the dream project. It was so named because it started off as a dream – an impossible dream. And the realization of this dream involves many people: a few of our visionary leaders, a dozen of government agencies & contractors, hundreds of our members and friends, and thousands of donors and supporters. I'd like to take this moment to thank each one of you, without your support, this dream project would still remain an impossible dream.

FCSN started in 1996 with ten families. Our mission is to help children with special needs and their families to find love, hope, and respect through community involvement. And our emphasis has always been on children, family, friends, and community. Those are our key words.

We can trace the start of Dream Project back to six years ago. In early 1999, FCSN was still a small organization with about 100 family members. At one of the board meetings, FCSN board of directors formed a task force to study the long-term goal for our organization. And the task force team, led by Linmei, my wife and president of FCSN at the time, came back to the Board with a proposal that was totally unexpected. The team described the proposed goal as a "dream community" where children with special needs can live and learn in an integrated environment, according to their abilities, with strong support from a community. The foundation of the plan is a community center which provides programs and support. I remember clearly that no one in the boardroom was ready to accept such an unrealistic goal. For a young organization, this was just a pipe dream. However, by the end of 1999, Albert Wang stood up and threw his support behind the project and formed a dream committee with Linmei and Peter Hsia. From that moment on, Albert took helm of the dream committee and led the team to define the scope of the dream project. He would become the FCSN president for three of the next five years and managed the project from the start to finish. His determination and drive were the key to the success of this project. He once said that to complete this project, we have to put in 110% of our effort; and I can testify, he has certainly done that.

So, how do you build a dream community from scratch with private funding? For a year, the committee studied all sorts of different options. Then, in 2000, Albert learned of an opportunity to purchase a piece of land in Fremont. A decision needs to be made within weeks. The dream committee immediately organized a group of FCSN parents to form a separate company called Peralta Dream LLC (PDLLC) to purchase this lot in support of the dream project, and PDLLC would later donate part of land to FCSN to build the Center.

With the land secured, then came the daunting task of financing the construction. First, Albert ran an internal fund-raising campaign, to provide the seed money and hired VMWP as the architecture firm to start the planning & rezoning process. By the end of 2002, FCSN was ready for external fund raising, and Limin Hu showed up just in time to help with the first gala event which was a huge success. From 2003-2006, Limin & Albert organized three more galas and five fundraising concerts to help raise over two million dollars to fund the Center construction. It was an incredible feat. During this period, they have galvanized FCSN members towards a common goal. In the process of building a Center, they have also built a stronger organization.

While the construction was going on, FCSN program team was busy with the blueprint of the programs. Up to now, most of the FCSN programs are geared towards children with special needs. When special children grow up, the need for support does not stop when they reach 21. With the new Center, we have become a vendor of East Bay Regional Center and started two brand new programs to serve this adult population: 1) a supported living service, to provide assistance to adults who are in supported living program, and 2) an Adult Day Program (ADP) to provides living skills, social skills and vocational training for adults over the age of 22. ADP program also takes our kids out to job sites to work so they can contribute to society according to their abilities. As a matter of fact, a few of our special adults will start working at Walmart next week. In the future, we plan to offer more integrated playgroups, therapeutic programs and after school programs. When we get all these programs running, we will be able to provide better support to our children and adults with special needs, and we will be a step closer to realizing our dream.

We all have had dreams before. Many of our members, including myself, are immigrants and first-generation Americans. We came to the Silicon Valley, the land of innovation, in search of a dream of prosperity and better lives for our children. But for some of us, that dream was broken when we found out that our children have disabilities. But together we found hope and built an organization and formed a big family, and our leaders dared to dream the impossible. Over the last few years, this Dream project has become our new American dream, and we are proud that it is finally realized in California, in Silicon Valley, in the city of Fremont.

# CARE TO SHARE

## Chenming Hu (FCSN Parent), Dec 2006

**Music camp was the first program to take place in the new Dream Center.
(summer, 2006)**

FCSN is building a supportive community where the children can live
and learn in an integrated environment. It functions as a transition
zone to the large and largely disinterested society. This is an excellent
model. I have seen its initial success.

In September, our son Raymond moved from Contra Costa
County into an apartment building next to the FCSN Center in order
to be close to the FCSN community. It is really touching for me to see
that two parents, Linmei and Jim Chiao, have sold their lovely home
in Cupertino and moved into this modest apartment building to be
the resident parents of all the children that live there. This kind of love
and devotion is the reason for the success of FCSN.

Margaret and I already see dramatic positive changes in Raymond. His skin is clear and he is happier, and there are other changes. Raymond has given me permission to share the following story with you.

I would like to tell you an incident that happened last weekend. Afterwards, I'll explain why I tell you the story. Raymond slept in our house on Friday night so that he and his mom could catch an 8am flight to Philadelphia from San Francisco the next morning. To be doubly safe, Margaret and I each set our alarm clock for 5am wake-up. The next morning, we were awakened by Raymond's voice. "Mom and dad, time to get up." First, we were confused. Then we saw bright day light through the windows, and we panicked. We looked at our clocks and realized what had happened. There was a power outage in the night and the alarms did not go off. "What time is it?" we asked Raymond. "Seven". "Seven o'clock? Why didn't you wake us up earlier?" Raymond was all dressed and ready himself. "But it's not late. The plane won't leave till eight!" We rushed to the car. I applied my speeding skills without guilt, and they caught their flight.

What is the point of this story? For as long as I can remember, it has been a daily struggle to get Raymond out of bed and out of the house in the morning. We pulled, pushed, pleaded, positively reinforced. Nothing worked. We consulted doctors. Sleep disorder was the diagnosis. Surgery was performed. Breathing machine was used at night. Still, Raymond didn't want to get up in the morning. This problem continued after he moved into an apartment in Walnut Creek three years ago. Magically, just weeks after he moved into the FCSN community, he now gets up bright and early in the morning, like last Saturday at our house, and sometimes even early enough to join other FCSN children in Tai Chi before breakfast. How can such a large change occur in such a short time? If you asked me, I'd say something changed in him, something profound and important. And we are very happy for him.

What exactly happened? My wife, Margaret, wrote an article for the June issue of the FCSN online newsletter with the title 'Thoughts on Parenting Children with Disability'. She shared several ideas. One of them is this. "We need to accept our children as they are, so that they will accept themselves." It seems to me that her statement applies to more than the parents. Not only the parents have to accept the children, but also a small community beyond the immediate families has to accept our children, then they will have happier lives, as Raymond does now.

In this small community that I am speaking of, it is as if all our children have large extended families – and all these families live in the same village. This gives the children a community where they are accepted as they are. The image of this village reminds me of the African proverb that Hillary Clinton popularized in the US: "It takes a village to raise a child." FCSN is building such a community. You are all part of this community. You are all invited to this village.

People in a village need places where they can get together and see one another. They interact in many activities that enrich their lives. Our community, the FCSN community, also needs physical spaces and activities for the children. Many of you have given FCSN financial support to help to build the FCSN Center in Fremont and to offer various programs to our children. Thank you for caring and sharing your fortunes with FCSN. However, the work is just beginning and we will need your continued support.

The first program that was offered in the new Center building was a summer music camp this past September. I was delighted to see quite a few children who are not Asian in the camp. I had not seen that number in previous FCSN programs. The Center also provides a base for offering services that qualify for government support, such as job training. This is how our community is being built, with your help, step by step, little by little.

If your financial support is the life blood of FCSN, and its founders and leaders are the brains, then the volunteers are the heart and soul of FCSN. The volunteers share their precious time after work or study and on weekends with our children. Our volunteers are teenagers, young adults, as well as not-so-young adults. They are siblings, parents, family. But mostly, they are just friends. They do everything. They are the leaders, teachers, helpers, cooks, janitors, parking directors, companions, playmates, and hand holders. Many of our children need one-on-one help in order to get exposure to arts, crafts, music, computers, reading, etc. There is a lot of work.

But the volunteers are more than just people who get the work done. Most people with special needs lack the skills to build a network of friends and this leaves a void in their lives. Parents know and academic studies have shown that special needs people consider the volunteers and staff as their friends, although the staff and the volunteers may view the children as clients or students.

You, the volunteers, are a vital part of the FCSN community. Your large number makes the FCSN community viable. You make this community – a community. Without you, FCSN is just a name and a building. We always need more volunteers.

On behalf of the FCSN parents, I would like to thank all the friends of FCSN, the F in FCSN, by presenting to you these words of Arthur Schopenhauer: "Compassion is the basis of morality." We take off our hats to you all. The 14th Dalai Lama wrote a book: "The Art of

Happiness". He gave this practical advice on happiness: "If you want others to be happy, practice compassion. If you want to be happy – practice compassion." I cannot say for sure that FCSN will make you any happier, (you look very happy already), but I surely want to say, "Thank you. Welcome to this village."

# CHAPTER 3:
# Build Our Dream
## (2007-2013)

The completion of our Fremont Dream Center construction in summer 2006 was a major milestone for FCSN. At the time, our co-chairman Albert Wang said it best: "The Center is our hardware, now we have to work on our software." By software, he meant the programs that can benefit our special needs families.

With James Chiao as president, FCSN hired several key staff for its operation during the year of 2006. First hired was Sylvia Yeh, who headed the new East Bay Adult Day Program. Then Linmei Chiao was tasked to head the new East Bay Supported Living Service. In addition, Lilian Lin, a volunteer at the time, was soon in charge of the finance department. With a handful of staff and a dozen clients, our East Bay programs were off to a good start. Last but not the least, Anna Wang, our volunteer VP, was nurturing the local programs in both East Bay and South Bay.

Started in 2007, Tsai-Wei became the volunteer president and stayed on for an incredible six consecutive terms (2007-2012). In 2008, FCSN expanded its operation in South Bay by opening a South Bay Center at World Plaza, Cupertino. In 2011, our South Bay Center found another temporary home at Taiwanese American Presbyterian Church in San Jose. Under Tsai-Wei's leadership and the management team, FCSN programs grew by leaps and bounds and the management system was firmly established. By 2013, with more than 800 family members, we had forty programs,100 staff, and served over 200 clients.

# THE DREAM PROJECT HAS BEGUN

## James Chiao (President 2006-2007), June 2007

FCSN's current and past presidents in 2006 (from left: Tsai-Wei Wu, Jim Chiao, Linmei Chiao, Anna Wang, Albert Wang, Limin Hu.)

Stepping up as president this last year was a daunting task. Following Albert is not easy under the normal circumstances, let alone in a year that has involved so many changes and growth for FCSN. Thankfully, Albert and Limin agreed to serve as co-chairmen while lending their abundant energy and talents to help bolster FCSN's growth.

And what a wonderful and exciting year it has been. After 5 years of planning, fundraising, and construction, our Dream Center was finally completed last summer. However, the completion of the Center only marked the beginning of our Dream Project – with the vision of building a community and a support network for our children and adults with special needs. The new FCSN Center is the foundation of our Dream Project, and it has made a tremendous difference for us. With this new home, we can plant the seeds to grow the programs to benefit children and adults with special needs. It is with this goal in mind that we have focused our energy and resources this year. During the past year, we have accomplished the following:

- Started the East Bay Adult Day Program (ADP), which has expanded to serve 24 consumers.

- Started the East Bay Supported Living Service (SLS), which now serves 8 consumers.

- Started the East Bay Family Support Gathering for over seventy families.

- Started numerous new local programs at the Center & in other cities

- Hired three program directors and added over fifteen new staff members.

- Added new volunteer functions such as volunteer coordinator, IT, and communications.

- Set up HR, Accounting, and office management functions.

- Completed major building improvements that include concrete walkway, phone system, computer network, storage sheds, audio system, office furniture, and new AC system.

- Held a wonderfully successful fundraising gala.

Under the leadership of program directors Sylvia Yeh and Linmei Chiao, along with excellent teachers and volunteers, we have established our vendorized programs at the Center. With the recent hiring of program director Nancy Eddy, we expect further growth in both ADP and SLS programs.

Even with much of the activities centered on the Dream Center in Fremont, we have managed to continue our family support gatherings in Saratoga, ADP in San Jose, and further expand our local programs in the South Bay cities. In addition, we expect a new program director to take over our south Bay ADP program in June.

Over a year ago, FCSN had only one full time employee. Within the last year, we have added three program directors, and fifteen more staff members. By setting up programs, functions, and more rigorous structures, FCSN has moved a big step from a volunteer organization to a more formalized organization. We will continue to grow in that direction while maintaining our volunteer's functions and spirit.

Personally, it has also been a truly remarkable year for my family and myself. Last summer, my son Brian graduated from a special ed. program in De Anza College and transitioned into the Adult Day Program at FCSN Center. My wife Linmei became a program director to launch the SLS program. To be closer to the Center, we also moved into the Peralta Apartment behind the FCSN Center. It is an experience that I have enjoyed and will cherish – watching the special needs adults doing the morning exercise, watching them walking to/ from the Center, and outings on Sundays. Living amongst our special adults taught me that they are really no different from the rest of us; and that the FCSN programs provide them with an opportunity to live an independent and healthy life in ways they are capable of. This small community is just an example of how the Dream Community can work.

Many volunteers have spent years in the planning and building of the Dream Center. And yet again, they were called upon to put in additional effort to build the programs for the Dream Project. I know saying "thank you" does not express my deep appreciation;

and I am in debt to all the FCSN officers, staffs, friends, supporters, donors, and volunteers for their contributions this year. Also, with a deeper understanding of the president's responsibility, I would like to thank all the past presidents of FCSN for their devotions. Finally, thank you all for giving me the opportunity to serve FCSN this year. Together, we can build a community of love, hope and respect for our special children.

# FCSN'S OUTLOOK IN 2008

## Tsai-Wei Wu (President 2007-2008), Feb 2008

Happy New 2008 to all FCSN members and community friends! Looking back the past years, 2006 was a monumental year for FCSN, because many of its long-incubated proje were finally completed or implemented. As a result, FCSN has entered into a new phase of growth – with the opening of our Dream Center in September 2006, FCSN East Bay operation no longer has to be conducted at borrowed or rented outside facilities, but can now host our activities at our own site; With the birth of our special adults programs, FCSN has progressed from being a parent-help-parent or parent-sharing type of services to becoming a state licensed service provider. All these major changes and astonishing accomplishments can only be attributed to our dedicated volunteers, staff, and administrative team plus the immense support from the community.

As of today, FCSN has launched three vendored programs, namely "East Bay Adult Day Program" (EBADP), "East Bay Supported Living Service" (EBSLS) in Fremont, and "South Bay Adult Day Program" (SBADP) in Cupertino. To maintain the operation and provide high quality services, FCSN has currently employed a total of 32 staff including one executive director, three program directors and four supervisors in the business sector. To further extend and improve our services in the South Bay area, we have been dedicating much effort and long hours in acquiring a facility so that a Center can be established in the South Bay.

The strategic direction in my tenure year will closely follow the same course that FCSN has laid down since 1996. In the organizational aspect, the administrative team is focusing on the future function development, operation infrastructure enhancement and program quality improvement. The team will also put more emphasis and resources in the volunteer sector to strengthen community involvement. Helping special needs kids/adults and their families are slated in the FCSN mission; FCSN Center is and will always be the place where these children and families can gain education, training, resources, comfort, and support.

Indeed, there are still tremendous challenges and huge amounts of work ahead of us. However, I strongly believe that with FCSN's committed volunteers, staff and administrative team all working together, we will be able to serve our community more effectively and productively.

**Selina Chih led a dance performance during our fundraising gala "Advance Our Dream". (2007)**

**Special needs adults performed during our fundraising gala "Advance Our Dream". (2007)**

# SIMPLICITY AND CHILDLIKE HEARTS

## Sylvia Yeh (East Bay Adult Day Program Director, LCSW), Feb 2008

**South Bay adult day program. (2008)**

A lot of friends ask me, "What is the Adult Day Program?", "Are you babysitting them while their parents work?", or "Why is FCSN ADP different from other day programs?" In order to answer these questions, I'd like to take you on a virtual tour to see how the developmentally disabled adults spend their time at FCSN East Bay Adult Day Program (EBADP).

When you enter FCSN, besides the spacious facility catching your attention, you will notice that the atmosphere is quite friendly and warm. You will be amazed at how enthusiastic and energetic the participants are when engaging in a variety of activities; how pure and delightful the participants' minds seem to be, and how caring, supportive, and dedicated the teachers are. EBDAP is run by a team of dedicated and experienced professionals. The staff ratio is 1:3 – all students get lots of attention and love. The main funding resource is RCEB

(Regional Center of East Bay). We are licensed by Community Care Licensing for 45 consumers, but currently we have thirty participants.

Vocational Training is the highlight of EBADP. We promote our participants to be productive contributors to the community. Our participants either work at a local store such as Wal-Mart or volunteer their time at the library and small businesses. We also have a diligent cleaning crew formed by five FCSN participants to keep the center clean and organized. The crew members receive compensation based on their job performance.

In music class, the participants sing loudly and happily. The melodies seem to bring a lot of comfort and joy to them. Even though their tone and pitch are not always the greatest and they're often not in tune, it still touches your soul to see that little seeds can blossom into gorgeous flowers.

In order to promote a healthy lifestyle, exercise plays a big role in the curriculum. It is carried out in different forms: line dancing, sports, yoga, walking around, etc. You can observe how hard the participants try to copy the movements of line dancing or yoga stretches despite some clumsiness or physical disability. You will then realize "dance like nobody's watching, love like you have never been hurt" is a blessing.

We also have weekly computer classes for students to sharpen their computer skills. Some of them learn to make PowerPoint presentations using lots of research and information, some learn to read through internet programs, some learn to maneuver the mouse or learn to type. No matter what levels they have, they are progressing at their own pace.

During Art & Craft and Drawing classes, participants use their fine motor skills to make awesome products. Through our creative teachers' instructions, participants fully concentrate to build projects, which makes them proud of themselves. Can you imagine that a balloon can turn into a piggy bank or wrapping tissue becomes a stylish hat? You have got to come and see.

We also focus on academic remediation on two subjects: Reading and Math. The participants tend to regress in their knowledge or skill if they don't have chances to practice. Some of them work on the reading and comprehension skills through chapter books, while others articulate phonics. For Math, we integrate math skills into daily life skills, such as learning to budget money before shopping. They also play board games to practice math skills.

One of the unique characteristics of FCSN EBADP are the field trips. We have been to many places in the Bay Area; for example: museums, East Bay Regional Parks, San Francisco, movie theaters, zoos, etc. For most places we have been to, we received informative and educational tours from the docents on sites. Our participants are very curious and adventurous. They are not afraid to touch and play with any hands-on exhibits. They interact with the docents, raise questions and make comments during field trips. They all seem to enjoy field trips very much, as they express excitement about any trip they've been on.

FCSN East Bay Adult Day Program provides comprehensive skill building activities and training to adults with developmental disabilities. Through abundant instruction and support, participants learn skills which enable them to hopefully live a fairly independent life, to work and participate in the community.

After working at FCSN for a year, I am very thankful to be part of this big family. Through it, I see hope, grace, and light. This is a utopian land where people treat each other with love, hope, respect, and support. This is a place where people not only dream – they fulfill these dreams and carry them out. Through the participants of EBADP, I realize that simplicity leads to happiness. I also witness that a childlike heart is the key to God's kingdom.

**FCSN EBADP Walmart team receiving a donation check from Walmart. (2008)**

# UNIQUE FCSN SUPPORT LIVING SERVICES

## Nancy Eddy (East Bay Support Living Services Director), Feb 2008

Supported Living is available from many different agencies; however, FCSN is unique in what it offers. Our commitment to the families of adults with disabilities as well as to the consumers themselves makes us special – we truly are a village providing care for our adult children. The program provides staff support for adults with disabilities in order for them to live an independent life as similar to any other adult as possible. The entire family is encouraged to be actively involved in developing that independence for their loved one.

Currently there are ten consumers that we provide services for living in five different apartments. Generally, each apartment has two or three roommates with disabilities and an able-bodied staff member living as an additional roommate in the four-bedroom apartments. Other staff work additional shifts so that, in most cases, 24-hour supervision is provided. Some consumers are growing into more independence and may not need 24-hour care so their staffing would be less.

Our goal is for each consumer to live as independently as possible with the ability to make their own decisions, have friends and lead as full a life as they can. There are many opportunities for the consumer to participate in social and sporting activities after their day program or work. It is the decision of the individual consumer as to what they are interested in. Opportunities include: Special Olympics, special trips to sporting events, musical events, local attractions and vacations, shopping, going to the gym, music or art classes, parties.

# PARENTS ARE MIRACLE WORKERS

## Anna Wang (VP of Programs), Dec 2008

### *An Amazing Year of Growth in Services*

What an exciting year at our flourishing FCSN village! We are blessed to have over 100 special families and volunteers joined forces with us. New and unique family support programs were launched. Our 30 existing programs were strengthened with the best teachers and therapists in both the East Bay and the South Bay. All these programs are parent-driven and designed to meet the needs of the families.

It is our goal to:

- Promote children/adults' independence, help develop permanent friendship among themselves, and explore their hidden talents.

- Provide fun learning opportunities usually not offered to children/adults with special needs.

- Help individuals with special needs to improve functioning level and develop self-help, life skills, and self-esteem.

- Empower families through support groups, seminars, workshops, and networking.

- Reach out to more individuals with special needs and families, especially Asian families, through our affordable programs.

FCSN currently has over 600 families with 60% of our members in the Santa Clara County. The South Bay families longed for a place to call home. And finally, with the birth of the New Center in Cupertino/ West San Jose, our prayers were answered. The Center allows us to replicate our successful programs from the East Bay and create brand new ones. While our directors were still working out the details of the lease, parents came together to form the South Bay Parents Steering Committee/ Core Team. Together, we produced several high-quality programs for our children and families. They are the Kinder Therapy Program, the South Bay Afterschool Program, the Full-Day Summer Camp, and the Mom's Club.

In May, the Kinder Therapy Program was born. This program improves youngest children's development and functioning level through different therapies. Since music is the universal magical language that work wonders with our children, Music Therapy is the first component to be included. Many of our children have deficits in sensory and motor skills; therefore, Occupational Therapy is a must in the program. The last component of Art Therapy fosters their creativity and exercises their fine motor muscle. We fully understand that two hours of these important activities for our young children would not be enough. Therefore, the Kinder Therapy Program is also a parent empowerment program. The program requires the parents to stay in the class and learn the activities so that they can conduct them throughout the week with their children at home.

The second program launched at the South Bay Center was the Pilot Afterschool Program. It was modeled after the successful Full-Time Afterschool Program at the East Bay Center. This program is designed to meet the needs of many families. Besides helping our children with academics and homework through our excellent teachers and wonderful high school volunteers, there is a special theme activity for each school day. These theme classes are taught by some of the best teachers and therapists of the field; social skills training, yoga for kids, art therapy, Shao-Lin Temple Kung Fu training, healthy cooking, and music therapy are among them. Our families have the choice to enroll their children in any or all of the theme classes or the entire afterschool program which runs from 3:00pm – 6:00pm. We accept school bus drop off. This well-package program has all the built-in activities that every parent would want for their own children. The Full-Time Afterschool Program is especially beneficial to families with both working parents who do not have time to take their children to the different classes.

Summer is a fun time for families but it's also a worrisome time. With school being out, most parents would still like their children to engage in activities that enrich their lives and enhance their growth. Our South Bay Parents Team is most daring to produce the first Full Day Summer Camp, operating from 9:00am through 6:00pm. The children enjoyed fun classes, such as, drum/percussion, exercise obstacle course, games, computer, yoga and kung fu. In the program, we also offered group speech therapy, academic maintenance, life skills and pragmatics training, and exciting field trips and exploration to local parks. Parents are welcomed to participate and assist in the Summer

Camp. What a blessing it is for the families to have such a great combination of recreational and educational activities as an option for the children!

Last but not least, our South Bay Center has a wonderful program for the wonderful ladies in FCSN. "Mom's Club" is a place where mothers can relax, share tears and joy, and take pleasure in each other's company. Currently, we meet every Wednesday morning and enjoy yoga together. Please come join us!

I have highlighted the new South Bay programs, but East Bay also started many magnificent programs this year. The new integrated playgroup funded by Every Child Counts, First 5 Alameda County, for our children ages 0 through 5 years, is extremely popular with a 6 months waiting list. Health is an important focus in our programming. The Center for Disease Control and Prevention indicated that 80% of adults with special needs are either overweight or obese. To prevent this health problem, our children really need lots of exercise and activities daily. This summer, we teamed up with Club Sport to host our first Basketball Camp and private Swim Lessons, in addition to our Soccer Camp, Music Camp, yoga and kung fu. All these programs make FCSN's support for families more comprehensive.

We applaud the great accomplishments of our families, volunteers, and paid staff for making our programs so special and successful. We look forward to expanding services to the Greater Bay Area. With your support and friendship, we are bringing our dream of our supportive village to the entire Bay Area closer and closer to reality.

# EXPANDING OUR DREAM TO SOUTH BAY CENTER

## Tsai-Wei Wu (President 2008-2009), Dec 2008

Happy New Year to all FCSN members and Families!!! Last year, I shared with you our commitments to excellence and our three strategic directions: Future Function Development, Operation Infrastructure Enhancement and Program Quality Improvement. Before we migrate to the new 2009, I would like to report to you, "Yes, we did it!! Our business administration team and volunteer staff members have made big strides towards our goals." Here are some highlights:

For Operation Infrastructure Enhancement, we have established a Human Resources system, an impeccable and transparent accounting operation, an upgraded IT system, and a brand-new database system in its beta-testing phase.

For Program Quality Improvement, East Bay Adults Day Program (EBADP) is one of our big success stories. It made a strong and steady growth; it has already reached its maximum capacity of 45 consumers in August this year. South Bay Adults Day Program (SBADP) has improved its facilities significantly and is much better equipped to embrace its future expansion. East Bay Supported Living Services (EBSLS) offers many job training sessions and skill enhancement workshops for our caregivers. The Independent Living Services (ILS) program is finally on its way and is now off to a good start.

On the children education program front, we improved our class curriculum and hired reputable Special Ed professionals in our East Bay (EB) and South Bay (SB) bi-weekly Family Support Gatherings. For family socials and bonding opportunities between members, our special event "Picnic in the Park/Sports Day" is back by popular demand. We also had a big joyful family camping trip at Mr. CC Yin's ranch in Vacaville this summer.

For the Future Function Development: We focus on local and after-school program development. We believe that the local program format is the most effective way to address the needs of the community, in terms of service breadth and suitability.

FCSN local program sector is part of FCSN's legacy and has been in operation for the past twelve years. Currently we have more than thirty local programs located throughout the Bay Area. One of our relatively young programs is our FCSN Afterschool program, launched in 2007 at the FCSN Fremont Dream Center. After nearly two years of hard work, the East Bay Afterschool program has established a solid infrastructure, and a stable yet diversified curriculum to help each student reach his or her highest potential. The content of the classes just gets richer and richer every day.

Since the birth of our Fremont Dream Center, the local/afterschool programs which were originally scattered throughout the East Bay, are now centralized in one location. Running our programs at our own facility certainly offers greater ease and flexibility.

On the contrary, without a place to call home, our South Bay operation was not so lucky. There were much more facility constraints and limitations. Our South Bay local programs were geographically located in the public facilities, such as YMCA, church sites, our members' living rooms or even garages. When comparing the FCSN program development between the East Bay and the South Bay, we could clearly see that the bottleneck for developing an equivalently, high quality afterschool program in the South Bay was due to not having our own Center there.

To have a "FCSN South Bay Center" was not a new idea at all. We fully understood this great need; it had been discussed internally for years. Our administration would like very much to realize the South Bay site this year and to promote more quality programs in the South Bay. When there is a will, there is a way!! With great dedication from our administrative team, motivation and momentum from our parents and volunteers, success came at last "The Birth of FCSN South Bay Center."

At the beginning of this year, we heard that a music studio in the World Journal Plaza on South De Anza Blvd was available for lease. The administration team immediately jumped on the case and acted on it: Upon verification, the FCSN office immediately proposed the

South Bay site development plan at the board meeting on 1/27/08 and obtained full support from the Board. Two task force teams were then formed: The "South Bay Site Administration" team led by Ivy Wu, former FCSN Executive Business Director, and the "South Bay Program Development" team led by Anna Wang, currently FCSN VP of Program.

The Administration team was in charge of lease/contract negotiation, use-permit application and all legal issues associated with the project. The Program team targeted to form a South Bay Core Parent group, integrated existing South Bay Local programs, and designed and formulated all the logistics of the South Bay after school program.

Besides those two task force teams, we appointed Kevin Lin, our construction coordinator, to direct all facility remodeling and construction projects at the new center. Since timing was critical, Kevin kept everything on a tight schedule and was able to meet the projected timeline. On 4/20/08, the Administration office reported back at the Board meeting that the South Bay Center was completed and ready to move in. The South Bay "Kinder Therapy Program" was the first local program launched at the South Bay Center on 5/4/08.

The birth of the FCSN South Bay Center itself was already a very impressive accomplishment; however, the story did not stop there. Due to our dedicated South Bay Core parents and FCSN staff, the team launched numerous pilot programs. They were then followed by the full-time afterschool program. They even successfully ran a two-week long South Bay Summer Camp in August, a very courageous move indeed.

In light of FCSN Gala2008 main theme "Expanding Our Dream" I am proud to introduce the FCSN South Bay Center to all our members and families. I would like to invite you to visit our South Bay

Center. With your continuing support, I know our South Bay operation will be doing great; With the SB Center, we can meet the needs better, and offer an even broader array of programs and services to the community.

Thanks to you all for helping FCSN be successful in 2008.

**FCSN opens South Bay Center at World Journal Plaza, and Anna organizes Mother's gathering at our SB Center (2008)**

# FCSN'S PROGRESS AND DEVELOPMENT

Tsai-Wei Wu (President 2009-2010), July 2009

First of all, my best wishes to you and your families, and hope you all have a wonderful summer.

Undoubtedly, the year 2009-2010 is financially tough for almost every nonprofit organization, particularly, for those which are heavily relying on the government funding, and FCSN is no exception. We are already affected by the previous three percent funding cutback and anticipating more cuts from the two local regional centers. However, the FCSN administrative team will do everything possible to sustain our normal operations in both the Business and Volunteer sectors.

To line up with the environment, all of our business programs are securitizing their expenditures more than ever. Our finance department is watching closely the overall financial performance and keeping the executive office fully informed the situation in a timely fashion. I strongly believe that, with our current resources and the support from our members and community friends, FCSN should be able to pull through this economically down time and continue fulfilling our commitments to the community.

In the year 2008-2009, the FCSN administration team has worked hard towards the three objectives/ goals which I committed two years ago, namely the Organization Infrastructure Enhancement, Program Quality Improvement and Future Function Development. I would like to take this opportunity to briefly update you what we have accomplished in the past year.

## Organization Infrastructure Enhancement

There are three key elements that compose a sound infrastructure, e.g., the People, System and Facility. On the People aspect, FCSN is always proud of its talented and devoted parent body. Parent power is always the main driving force to keep FCSN moving forward and it will always be. An excellent example is our South Bay (SB) Core Parent team, the team that has supported the SB volunteer program operation since FCSN SB Center was founded in 2008. In the business management side, after one more year's operation, I am proud to tell you that as of today FCSN has a much stronger, dedicated and coherent administrative team in place, and the team is ready to take on challenges.

On the System aspect, we have established an administration reporting chain which clearly defines staff's work scope, responsibility and accountability from top down. Furthermore, we have embedded a Quality Assurance mechanism in the daily operation so as to assure that service quality is warranted. We have also established a transparent, effective and audit-proven finance/accounting system, a versatile accounting flow process for tracking the SLS employee scheduling, and a balanced HR system to protect our employee legal rights and offer them a better benefit package.

On the Facility aspect, FCSN Fremont Center had collaborated with ChungHwa Telecom and Vicomtel to install an advanced VoIP/IT phone system at our Fremont Dream Center. This VoIP/IT upgrade has not only effectively solved our urgent needs in office phone services, but also provided ample IT capacity for our growth in the next five or more years.

In order to meet the office space demand for our growing office staff team, the Site-Op operation has established a well-equipped multi-function staff office in the Center Library and a small mobile office in the Nursing classroom. We are also very happy to see that our Candle Lighter $16,000 grant application has been approved, and very possibly, those deteriorated carpets in the classrooms will be replaced by the end of this year.

## Program Quality Improvement

Our East Bay Supported Living Services (EBSLS) department passed the East Bay Regional Center (EBRC) on-site audit with a high score in March! Our East Bay Adults Day Program (EBADP) passed the RCEB Self-Audit and CCL on-site inspection in late last year. Because our EBADP is so well received, the program has already exceeded its full capacity of forty-five consumers. EBADP is currently launching a new Community-Integrated Day Program (CIDP) in parallel to extend out ADP services beyond the maximum cap.

The South Bay Adults Day Program (SBADP) has reached 11x consumers and it is still growing steadily. With Kaiser Permanente grant, the ADP Department has launched a newsletter project to provide timely program info, activity reports, new nutrition findings and much more to our ADP community. In the past three months, the FCSN ADP Newsletter has demonstrated its rich content, high quality writing and publication consistency. It is one of significant achievements in our business operation.

In the volunteer sectors, the SB volunteer program has been the main focal point and we have launched SB local and After-School Programs since the SB site was founded in May 2008. Among those programs, the SB Kinder program is standing out, and because it is so successful, the program model has been replicated in our EB Local/After School programs.

Many grass-root types of tasks have been working on throughout the year by the Volunteer Program Division, those tasks include: publicizing FCSN & programs to attract more participants; providing and maintaining high quality for our Local, After-School programs, Bi-weekly Regular Gathering and Mother's Gathering; securing more funding to subsidize our volunteer programs, and evaluating the effectiveness of all the new programs. FCSN will continue maintaining a strong operation in the voluntary sector, because the latter is a crucial gateway for FCSN to serve the community.

## Future Function Development

In the year 2009-2010, the ADP Department will grow its CIDP and develop more On-site job training curricula in EBADP, the department will also continue creating more external job opportunities for both EB and SB consumers. FCSN will continue investing in SBADP because it is a key foundation for the future development of FCSN vendored programs in the South Bay. While enriching its program content, the SBADP will keep growing at its full speed and reach its 24x consumer target by the year end 2009.

The SLS/ILS programs are those programs which contain incredible complexities and challenges. We recognize that the job has never been easy and appreciate what the SLS/ILS team has accomplished as of today. On top of our current SLS/ILS achievements, we will pursue our continued improvement in the service quality: The near-term goal for EBSLS is to significantly improve parent communication, the midterm goal is to steadily improve SLS caregiver service performance, and the long-term goal, also as a measure to the SLS/ILS success, to earn our SLS/ILS parent's confidence.

Looking back FCSN's history, with the opening of our Fremont Dream Center in September 2006, FCSN was able to consolidate EB operations/activities at a self-owned location. Furthermore, FCSN was able to launch center-based types of vendored programs for the EB adults with special needs. As a result, FCSN has become a state licensed service provider and created a business sector on top of its volunteer basis.

Similarly, with the opening of our South Bay Center in May, 2008, FCSN SB operation also entered a new phase of operation: Namely, we have created a home for the FCSN SB families, promoted FCSN SB parents' morale, launched center based SB Local and After-School programs and provided a much better facility support to our SBADP. The SB operation has been benefited quite a lot from the Center site located in the World Journal Plaza, however, it is also restricted by the limited facility as well, e.g., not a perfect location for the After-School program development, insufficient classroom/office spaces, lacking kitchen facility, etc. In other words, if FCSN is planning to have an equivalent operation between EB and SB, then definitely the SB will need a larger, better, and self-owned center site for the long run. The year 2010 will be a pivotal year for FCSN South Bay development.

In summary, the 2008-2009 year overall was a good year, the FCSN team has got lots of things done. More importantly, FCSN has established a stronger, healthier and better equipped infrastructure, has placed an experienced and coherent administrative team, has locked a Quality Assurance mechanism to the management system, and has integrated the job procedure, performance requirement together with a vertical supervising chain to standardize the front-line service quality. I am confident that our administration team will be more efficient and productive in the coming years.

# DISABILITY CAPITOL ACTION DAY

## Ingrid Cheng (ADP Instructor), Jul 2009

On May 27th, 2009, a group of FCSN children, parents, Adult Day program students, teachers and volunteers (total of 44 people) embarked on a trip to the capital city of California – Sacramento – to advocate against the budget cuts laid upon the special needs and disabled communities of this state. Led by Anna Wang, one of the founders of FCSN, they took the almost two-hour long trip by FCSN chartered bus to the hot, bright sunshine setting in front of the capitol building.

Fortunately, there was ample shade in which FCSN set up a tent and took a breather before taking up signs to protest. There were a lot of other people there with the same cause, many with special needs and physical disabilities. In front of the capitol steps, speakers shouted their opposition and begged the government to think of the people; one man spoke on behalf of his sister, another on behalf of himself even though his speech was difficult to understand. A large American flag shone glittering behind the podium and everyone present rallied.

Several FCSN families gained access into the capitol building to testify at a hearing on the proposed budget cut. At the hearing, people who had special needs and disabilities, family members, as well as those advocating for these people, lined up to testify. There were so many people, they had to limit the testimonies to ninety seconds each and only one or two representatives per organization. Anna Wang testified on behalf of the 600 families in FCSN. Our South Bay member, Jennifer Timmermann, testified for the hundreds of parents of children with Autism and Asperger. Both of them explained the financial and emotional hardship that all the families experienced. With the devastating cuts to the Regional Center and the Developmental Services, parents lost all hopes for their children and families. Many of them are contemplating suicide. Anna sited two cases, one in Southern California, and one in Northern California, that a couple of single parents were so depressed about their situations that they committed murder-suicide, killing their children with disabilities and then taking their own lives. Many parents felt that the lack of compassion and the short-sightedness of "saving today and letting tomorrow takes care of itself" attitude, led to the heartless cuts and elimination of essential services to the disability community. Parents fear that their children will end up being institutionalized which will cost so much more for the State and the society at large. Two of FCSN's adults – Cindy and Jocelin – testified at the public hearing as well. They gave a brief look into their lives as roommates, who are able to have a home and jobs through services provided and supported by the Regional Center of the East Bay. How would their lives become different if they were forced to give up the support and services, due to the budget cuts. Others spoke about the richness and level of independence, achievement, service and learning that came from government support. Individuals received access to programs (such as day programs, like FCSN) where they learned a vocational trade, participated in activities which filled their lives with richness and became a part of a community which loved and cared for them.

Individuals receive utilities which help them with their daily lives and made them independent and functional in society. One young man with cerebral palsy, whose arms were twisted and unusable and who was unable to speak, was able to talk to the gathered masses by using a computer voice system; he proficiently typed out his speech with his feet into the machine, which in turn translated his text to spoken word. As a taxpayer, a voter, a human being – this man made it clear that budget cuts would devoid him of these daily tools and means in which he could go about his lives.

In fact, if it were not for the support from the government, many special needs and disabled people would be in state hospitals and large-scale facilities. This would break the hearts of so many families; and many parents fear that the lives of many would become void, and more stagnant.

Through testifying in the capitol building and through rallying out in front of the building, FCSN let their voices be heard that day in Sacramento. Renee, one of the FCSN ADP students, lamented over how there might not be any more field trips or even a day program because of budget cuts. She stood up and booed the governor for even thinking about doing such a thing. Hopefully, for the sake of Renee – and for everyone affected – the government of California will find a way to stop these cuts to our communities.

Special thanks to Family Voices and CFILC for making this trip possible for our FCSN Community.

# ADVOCACY – OUR CHILDREN'S LIVES DEPEND ON IT!

## Anna Wang (VP of Programs), July 2010

**FCSN participated in a rally against budget cut in Sacramento (2010)**

It's becoming an annual tradition that FCSN organizes a busload of our children, adults, and family members to rally and testify at Disability Capitol Action Day in Sacramento.

The past several years has been so difficult for our community of people with disabilities and our families, community organizations and workers who provide support and services. Since late 2001, budget cuts kept growing in depth and spreading to other needed programs and services. Our Developmental Disability community never benefited from good times. But, when it came to budget cuts, we always ended up in the front of the line.

Year after year after year, we face threats of cuts or elimination of programs. We are deeply anxious, worried, and frightened about what is happening. People are scared to lose their homes, their services, their support, their jobs, and the paycheck that supports their families. The reduction or elimination in benefits and services such as IHSS, SSI/SSP, CAPI grant, mental health services, early intervention, respite, and direct care-services bring tremendous fear to our community. You can see it in their faces. You can hear it in their voices.

But for some of us who didn't get the cuts this time or somehow we are okay because the cut to us was rejected, we rest in a state of false complacency. One thing I can guarantee you is if we don't stop the cuts now, everyone will be hurt sooner than anyone anticipates. There is no safety in hiding behind a closed door or sanctuary. We are all threatened.

"We are tired of fighting, no one cares about us", one parent told me. Everyone in our community feels fatigue. But we can't keep quiet, or the governor and the legislators will think we have gone away, we don't exist anymore. We don't have a choice but to fight.

A country is judged by how they treat their most vulnerable citizens and how they respect human rights. California has turned into a third world country definitely with the way the system/legislators treat our people with special needs. We have to let them know that they are accountable for the lives of their disabled citizens. We won't give in. We won't go away! We won't go away! In fact, we have to be "IN THEIR FACE" as such as possible. Stand United with FCSN and say, "NO MORE CUTS, STOP KILLING US, HAVE A HEART"!! We have to continue this fight for our children and be the voice of our loved ones. THEIR LIVES DEPEND ON IT!!!"

# EMPOWER OUR YOUTH WITH WEP

## Tsai-Wei Wu (President 2010-2011), July 2010

Dear FCSN Members and Friends,

How are you! First of all, wish you all a wonderful summer season. Undoubtedly, the year 2009-2010 continues to be a financially challenging period for many nonprofits, especially ones that rely heavily on government funding. Fortunately for FCSN, our devoted staff, parents, volunteers, friends and community partners have helped us make this tough year into a productive year. I would like to take this opportunity to thank you for making FCSN better and stronger.

I am very pleased to report that the FCSN Business sector has grown its consumer base from 79 to 113 this year, a significant growth of 43%. During the same period, we have also increased our employee headcounts from 53 to 71. If we include the 37 contractors employed by our Volunteer sector, FCSN is already a 100-employee organization today, not to mention our 600+ family members.

The Adults Day Program (ADP), led by Vivian and Sylvia, launched the East Bay Community Integrated Day Program (EB CIDP) in June 2009. It started with only 10 students and grew incredibly. It reached its maximum student capacity of 24 in just nine months. As of today, the CIDP has 25 students and there are still 15 more students on the waiting list. Sylvia and her team have requested East Bay Regional Center to consider further increasing our student capacity to 36 so we can bring this excellent service to more people. The high demand for our East Bay CIDP has confirmed that FCSN provides one of the best services in the community.

One year ago, I promised to improve our Supported Living Services/Independent Living Services (SLS/ILS) programs and extend services to the South Bay. Since then, the East Bay SLS/ILS started a quality assurance project by Nancy and Rebecca. They re-structured SLS Case Managers, provided many workshops and training, established comprehensive documentation on worklist, check-list, implementation procedure, and weekly communication with our SLS/ILS parents. All those QA measures have shown great effectiveness and earned good marks with our SLS/ILS families. However, our work is not yet complete. Our next step is to further strengthen the training of our direct care staff. I anticipate a complete QA project evaluation around the end of the 3rd quarter this year.

There is significant growth in our South Bay ADP. The program started with 11 students last year and has grown to 16. Vivian and her team have done an excellent job in enhancing the program content and improving its quality. Many parents expressed high praises for the program.

To deliver great services, qualified staff is the key. Therefore, our business team recruited good people and provided them with well-defined work procedures, adequate supervision, and job skills training.

We held two intensive training workshops in March and April this year, where over 90% of the staff members expressed the great benefits of such training for their daily work. Also, 100% of FCSN staff agreed or strongly agreed that "It is pleasant to work at FCSN." I consider this a wonderful accomplishment from our business management team, since when we have happy staff, we have happy consumers.

One year ago, FCSN established an integrated financial/accounting infrastructure to serve both the Business and Volunteer sectors. In the past year, Lilian and her team further strengthened FCSN with an HR infrastructure that has broadened our general logistics supporting functions. They built a solid foundation for FCSN's sustainability. Furthermore, Lilian and her team are all part-time employees. However, what they have contributed to FCSN far exceeds any full-time professionals. They really deserve a big applause and our deepest appreciation.

There are many accomplishments from our Volunteer Program sector as well. One year ago, I declared that 2009-2010 is the Year of the South Bay. One year later, our South Bay core parent team handed in a brilliant report card. Besides continuing the highly successful Kinder (Candy/coordinator), Dance (Shu-Ling/coordinator) and Basketball (Sherry/coordinator) programs, the team added the Art/Ceramic (Kaili/coordinator) and Life skills training (Sherry/coordinator) programs to the list. Our volunteer programs are better than ever, and our parent team, most commendable.

The South Bay core parent team has gone through a rough year. Our beloved South Bay program coordinator, MaLi, took a sudden leave due to health reasons. Her absence impacted the South Bay deeply because of her multiple roles in the team. However, our core parents really acted as a big family and united at this crucial moment: Jenny jumped right in and took care of the South Bay local program coordination; Kaili extended her after school program coordinator role for a few more months, and later launched a new Saturday Art/ Ceramic class program; Candy took over the FCSN Newsletter task and Marta handled the Kinder program. Our core team worked together very closely and stretched themselves to keep programs running.

Through Anna's heavy involvement in the Developmental Disability (DD) Community and passionate advocacy for our children, Chi-Am Circle has generously funded FCSN with $30K to educate our teenagers with basic life skills, social skills, and vocational skills. The South Bay core team ingeniously combined the existing Life Skill program with work skills training to become a Work Empowerment Program (WEP) for our teenagers with special needs. Sherry Meng first introduced this class at the South Bay Regular Family Support Gathering. Due to Sherry's excellent curriculum design, Shirley's motivating teaching style, and Cherene's logistic support, the program was highly successful and has become the most popular class in the Gathering.

Our success story did not end here. Due to Anna's grant writing efforts and advocacy for FCSN, the Volunteer Sector has received a total of $167.6K of grant funding in 2009-2010. This is an incredible feat for such a financially challenging year. We owe many thanks to Anna's tireless endeavor.

Overall, the Year 2009-2010 is a good year for us, because the big FCSN family has made solid strides toward a stronger, healthier, and better structured organization. The Year 2010-2011 will be another productive year, because FCSN has added the following values:

- A stable and experienced administrative team ready to face any challenge.

- A Quality Assurance mechanism embedded in the infrastructure.

- A continuous job skills training program to ensure and to maintain the quality of our staff.

- Momentum building up in the South Bay.

South Bay core parent team has accomplished so much, South Bay ADP's growth and SLS/ILS's deployment are very successful, and MaLi is coming back to join forces in August. Riding on this tremendous momentum, we are ready to achieve our wishes of establishing our South Bay Dream Center. Therefore, our 2011 focus will still be in the South Bay!!!

I am fully confident that FCSN will bring more success stories to share with you in the coming year. Thank you all and we are looking forward to working closely with you!!!

# LIFE SKILL TRAINING CLASSES

## Sherry Meng (Parent and Board member), July 2010

As parents, we dream that our children can someday live independently, hold a job and have a happy life. To reach this goal, we need to help them prepare. At the beginning of 2009 summer, SB parent leaders decided to open a life skills training class. I was assigned to design this class.

At first, I did a survey to see what the parents wanted. After a summer of research, I decided to focus on training personal independence skills first. An important part of personal skills is cleaning up.

For our "clean up" lessons, each child needed to sweep the floor using sweeper. We spread flour on the floor to help students identify dirty areas. Youth volunteers guided them to do the job. They also set up the big tables and learned how to wring dishrags and wipe the tables. We also taught them how to set a table using a placemat that showed where to put their plates, forks, knives, spoons, and cups. They peeled bananas and cut them to small pieces using a knife. They served themselves with the fork. After eating, they cleaned up their own things and put the tables and chairs back. In later sessions, students also made jelly sandwiches. Also, we taught them to use different containers to pour water.

The result was great, and the students enjoyed the work as well. Considering that some kids can finish everything quickly, we asked them to help teachers put all the tools back. We also brought some outside jobs to the class. For example, students helped the Kumon center to fold their advertisements.

We also did a car wash. The children learned how to wash the car, soap the car, rinse the car, dry the car, and clean the windows. We washed a total of four cars that day. The adult class washed one car in ten minutes at the end. The cars were very clean, and everyone was happy. We hope that we can do this kind of activity every semester.

Throughout this semester, the feedback from teachers, students and parents were positive. Our kids liked to do the work. Also, a group class is a good way to teach basic life skills. The kids were more cooperative and followed instructions well. It is very similar to our children learning Chinese; we all can teach them, but most of time we still send them to Chinese school. This is because we need consistency and a good learning environment. But still, parents can help greatly by practicing these skills with their children at home. It will help them to master these skills quicker.

Next semester, we will continue using the same teaching strategy – breaking down the procedures step by step, then using a demo to show them how execute the skill. Using visual aids and hand to hand help will help them learn better.

For next semester, we would like to set different level skills with different groups. For children older than fifteen, we would like to focus more on job related skills training. For children younger than 15, we will still work on their basic life skills.

In the semester we would like to introduce another personal independent skill – handling clothing. We will work primarily on caring for clothing. This includes sorting and folding different kinds of clothes, hanging them up based on categories, matching the socks, buttoning, and zipping clothes, and removing different stains. Also, we will teach them to organize their closets. Other clothing-related skills include making the bed and how to dress appropriately for different situations. If some students master these skills, we may introduce them to sewing buttons and ironing clothes.

There are many more life skills that can be taught: interpersonal skills, living skills, vocational skills, communication skills, problem solving skills and so on. I strongly hope that we can introduce more of these skills to our children. I hope that someday our children can live independently, enjoy their job and have a happy life.

# YAY! FCSN HAS A NEW HOME IN SOUTH BAY

## Vivian Chung (SBADP/EBCIDP Manager), July 8, 2011

**FCSN South Bay Center moved to a facility at TAPC site. (2011)**

We lost counts for how many properties that we had visited, how much time we had spent on searching for a new home. But now, all these aren't important anymore, because – We have found our NEW home! It is an office building of Taiwanese American Presbyterian Church located at **3675 Payne Ave, San Jose**, CA 95117.

The moment we walked into the facility, we fell in love with the indoor gym, fully equipped kitchen, large dining area, huge parking lot, roomy office space, green courtyard, quiet neighborhood, and the walkable distance to park and community center.

Since the facility was built long time ago, FCSN spent about three weeks to renovate and clean up our new home. At the same time, South Bay Youth and Adult program teachers and students helped to pack and clear out clutters from the old center. They were divided into groups and have different responsibilities. Some recycled scrap paper and newspapers, some shredded documents, some packed books, etc. FCSN Accounting Office and Site Operations helped to solve all logistic issues and supplies purchase.

All SBADP students and staff helped to pack and unpack the boxes for the move. They also cleaned the old facility, so we got the full security fund back from the previous landlord. Before they moved into the new site, the students worked hard in cleaning so we could have a good start. This is a very valuable experience for all of us. Not only that we have a new home, we have learned that we can achieve big thing when we are working as a team.

Though we have moved in for a month, we are still excited about it. There are cubbies for students to store their belongings, two big storage areas, art room with sink installed, comfortable computer room, an airy music/dance room and a nice common area.

Next time when you are in South Bay area, remember to visit us at our new home. Looking forward to seeing you soon!

**SBADP students play basketball at the indoor gym**

# IN-HOME RESPITE SERVICES

## Mannching Wang (South Bay program coordinator & youth volunteer coordinator), Oct 2011

### *FCSN becomes a new vendor of In-Home Respite Services through both SARC and RCEB*

FCSN has been working hard to provide services to our parents. Being a parents' non-profit organization, we always put our parents and our children's interests first.

Starting mid and late 2011, parents were no longer authorized by the Regional Centers as a Respite vendor. This change resulted in a lot of extra work for our parents. First, we needed to persuade our current respite providers to find an agency to accept them as respite workers/employees, obtain First Aid/CPR certificates, and run a fingerprint clearance. Since some of our care providers had language barriers, they chose to quit the job of providing service to our special needs individuals.

FCSN acted quickly after getting parents' feedback. Anna Wang and Sylvia Yeh worked hard to apply FCSN to be an In-Home Respite Service vendor through both SARC and RCEB, so that our parents could use their Respite service in an easy way and not worry about the paperwork.

If you desire FCSN to be your respite provider, you just need to make a phone call or email your SARC/RCEB case manager (the social worker) that you choose FCSN to be your respite service agency. Once POS is authorized, we will contact you to find out your preferences of the service time, and recruit a suitable respite worker for you at your home when you need a break and provide ongoing supervision and training to ensure quality of service. You don't need to do any paperwork or go through any complicated procedures.

What makes the FCSN respite program different from that of other respite agencies? Firstly, we know FCSN families' parents and their children. We can find good matching care providers to serve your child. Secondly, FCSN tries very hard to find high quality and reliable care providers, and give them adequate training before they go on the field. Lastly, we communicate well with parents and are open for parents' feedback.

We understand good care providers are vital, and allow you to feel comfortable when you leave your special needs child/adult at home. Therefore, we urgently ask you to refer people to apply for the position. If you know anyone who is interested in working with the special needs population, please encourage them to contact me (Mannching Wang) for SARC consumers or Maria Campos for RCEB consumers.

# CHAPTER 4:
# Spread Our Dream
## *(2014-2016)*

Ever since the construction of our East Bay Center in Fremont in 2006, our South Bay families had long looked to a day when they have a permanent center that they can call their own. Their dream finally got closer when FCSN purchased a property at S. Bascom Avenue in 2014...

In the following three years, the renovation of the South Bay Center took center stage at FCSN. With the Fremont Dream Project under our belt, FCSN was more experienced at handling this type of renovation project. The construction began in 2015, and our team included Albert/Anna Wang, Linmei/Jim Chiao, Sylvia Yeh, Stanley Woo, Jeff Woo, Charlene Liao, and Roxana Chu. We also got much needed volunteer help from Mandy Chang on the interior design, and David Tu on construction management.

# A TIME TO REFLECT & LOOK FORWARD

## James Chiao (President 2013-2014), June 2014

### *FCSN South Bay Center Property Purchased!*

FCSN site search committee, from left: Stanley Woo, Sy-Cheng Tsai(architect), Jim Chiao, Linmei Chiao, Albert Wang, Charlene Liao. (Sylvia Yeh absent)

## A Word about Our Newsletter

As president this year, I set as one of my goals to bring the FCSN Newsletter back to our members and friends. I have a fond memory of the very first issue of the FCSN newsletter: it was published in late 1996, when FCSN was just formed and registered as a business entity. We only had a small core group of member families and a volunteer-based planning committee. We did not have a president, board of directors, or staff of any kind. Nonetheless, we decided to publish a newsletter, and everyone chipped in to write articles, edit, print, collate, and bind. Sure enough, in February of 1997, we distributed the first issue to our loyal members. The publication continued for many years; however, in 2009, the publication came to a halt after our then chief editor Ma Li passed away after a bout with cancer. During the last few years, there was no shortage of other FCSN publications. For example, from 2010 to 2013, we had a publication from our ADP (Adult Day Program), with a limited distribution to ADP families. Today our Supported Living Service still publishes an SLS newsletter every six months. Additionally, Anna Wang has continued to make her regular email announcements. What has been missing is a publication that represents a cross-section of our community where we can hear voices from our members, staff, volunteers, and people with special needs – exactly what the FCSN newsletter was meant to provide. Publishing the newsletter was not a big task back then, yet it has always been one of those projects that bring families together.

## Developing Our Culture

This year, we have seen relatively little growth except in the ILS (Independent Living Service) program. This comes after seven years of fast growth since the center was built in 2006. Why so little growth this past year, you may be wondering. There are several reasons: most of our vendored programs are capacity limited and the restricted funding from Regional Center did not help. FCSN has grown so fast these last seven years; there are some growing pains that need to be addressed. Luckily, this year is turning out to be a good time for us to take stock in our organization. At the board level, we embarked on a journey of soul searching; we wonder how best to state our mission. We pondered our direction. We realized that beyond setting business goals and objectives, we also need to establish our culture. We spent a lot of time in the boardroom, discussing our culture and how to develop it. One thing that shapes our culture and reflects FCSN is our core values – this is why we initiated a core value survey among our staff and members. It is important to look at all these factors to emerge a cohesive view before we expand and enter into the next phase of our development.

Over the past six months, FCSN board and key managers have discussed and selected a list of seven possible core values which we believe best fit our organization. These core values were not chosen at random; in fact, they were chosen based on what we believe and from our many years of experience working within this organization. For example, the first core value "Dare to Dream" can be traced directly to our experience in the Dream Project. In 2000, when the Dream Project was first proposed, very few people believed in our dreams of building a community center for our children and adults with special needs. I still remember the moment when we first visited the open lot on Peralta Boulevard, and three managers – Albert Wang, Linmei Chiao, and Peter Hsia – made the decision to purchase the property. At the time I thought the plan was outrageous and risky. However, within two weeks, over twenty FCSN families joined in to make it happen. Eventually, part of the land was donated to FCSN to build our community center which is now the cornerstone of our community. The bottom line underscoring this core value is this: "If we don't dream for our children with special needs, who will?"

## South Bay Center Site Search Accomplished!

When FCSN started in the South Bay in 1996, we moved our meeting location from place to place over the years. In 2010, FCSN moved our main South Bay operation to the rented facility at TAPC church which became our SB Center. However, it has always been our desire to find a permanent home in the South Bay. The reason is simple. One of our goals is to build a permanent community center, and we cannot build a community center on borrowed land. Once a community center is created, many adults and families with special needs can find permanent housing near the center. However, finding the right site is no easy task given the constraints of location, zoning, and cost. Within FCSN, this task was the responsibility of the site search committee, led by Dr. Albert Wang. After searching for the last three to four years, we expanded our search criteria this year and doubled our efforts. Luckily, with the help from board member Stanley Woo, we finally found a property on South Bascom Avenue that met our requirements: it is conveniently located, near the center of San Jose, and easily accessible from all directions in the South Bay. It is close to the new Bascom Community Center and San Jose City College where many of our ADP students attend school. In addition, it's near a nice neighborhood, where housing may be available to our special adults. After the search committee conducted a few weeks of due diligence, I am proud to announce escrow closed on April 7th, 2014, and FCSN has become the new owner of the property. Now, the team is working with architect Sy-Cheng Tsai to start the design process. Within a few months, we will have a better idea of the design and construction timeline.

## Looking Ahead

By strengthening the infrastructure for volunteer and family support, we can build a stronger foundation for the FCSN community. With a strong foundation, we can add more programs to provide a village of support for our children with special needs. With the purchase of the South Bascom property, we are poised for a new chapter in FCSN. We expect to replicate and expand upon the successful Dream Center/

Community model we established in the East Bay. Our vision of building a dream community is clear and resonates with our members and families. With everyone's support, I am sure we can realize our vision of a better tomorrow for our children and families.

# DREAM PROJECT 2

## Anna Wang (Vice President of Local Programs), June 2014

### *Dare to Dream the Impossible Dream Again?!*

The FCSN community wants our special needs loved ones to have happy, healthy, and fulfilled lives. In the year 2000, FCSN embarked upon the first Dream Project, uniting FCSN families and supporters to achieve our dream of building a visual model of a supportive village. This system consisted of our center for programs, with nearby housing for living and support services. Today, we are looking at the fruits of the labor of Dream Project team members. FCSN has two centers, one in Fremont and one in San Jose, serving more than 800 families through over 40 programs/services, with more than 200 volunteers and 100 staff members. The power of love for our loved ones is behind the success of our Project. We are humbled that many Bay Area organizations look to FCSN to learn from our model of support.

As more of our children have become adults or are approaching adulthood, family members are beginning to worry about their children's prospect of finding work in the community. National reports indicate that merely 12.5% of our population with developmental disabilities has any kind of job and only 1% has full-time employment with competitive wages. Are we going to accept this? ARE WE GOING TO ACCEPT THIS? NO. The FCSN community will NOT stand for this. We have to do something about it!

In November 2012, Dream Project 2 was launched. It's all about "Building a Brighter Future for Our Loved Ones with Special Needs" by preparing them for the work force and providing them job opportunities.

# The objectives of Dream Project 2 are:

- Explore Talent, Interests and Abilities
- Promote Self-Esteem by Setting Them Up for Success
- Provide Competitive Wages
- Ensure Protection from Bullying and Abuse
- Offer Job Security and Satisfaction
- Engage in Scheduled Positive Productive Behavior

Strategies

a. Train children at home and at FCSN programs so they are prepared

b. Assess their Abilities and Talents

c. Create Career Opportunities by:

- Finding employment through the parents' network with businesses
- Parents forming businesses to offer tailor-made job for their own adult children
- FCSN acting as Fiscal Managers to create business entrepreneurship
- FCSN collaborating with businesses to offer jobs to our adult day program students

Current projects in progress are:

1. Senior Community Housing Project
2. Organic Bath & Beauty Products
3. High-End Chocolate Project
4. Special Needs Entrepreneurship and Business Service Contract

5.  Computer-Related Employment

Things won't happen unless we make them happen. We are family members and friends, the stakeholders who have vested interest in the success of the project(s). It's not too late to join us. Please contact Auntie Anna and sign on.

Together, we can make all our Dreams Come True!

# INTRODUCTION OF FCSN VENDORIZED PROGRAMS

Sylvia Yeh (Executive Business Director), June 2014

**Community Integrated Day Program (CIDP) in Fremont Area. (2014)**

FCSN parents pondered what their children with special needs would do after exiting the educational system. How could parents ensure that their children would continue to learn and grow more independent and productive without the structure of an educational system? Parents wondered how FCSN could support and enrich their lives continuously. These questions and the Dare-to-Dream mentality resulted in FCSN pursuing adult services with California Regional Centers. In 2004, FCSN started an Adult Day Program (ADP) in the South Bay. In 2006, after FCSN launched its headquarters in Fremont, FCSN expanded its service programs, becoming a vendor of Adult Day Program and Supported Living Services (SLS) with both San Andreas Regional Center (SARC) and Regional Center of the East Bay (RCEB). FCSN further pursued vendorization for respite services in 2011.

## Adult Day Program

FCSN currently operates three adult day programs: East Bay Adult Day Program (EBADP), Community Integrated Day Program (CIDP), and South Bay Adult Day Program (SBADP). EBADP and CIDP are located in Fremont and SBADP in San Jose. With the goal of promoting independence and personal growth, FCSN adult day programs are set to provide holistic training in the areas of:

- Vocational Skills/Job Readiness
- Academic Remediation
- Healthy Lifestyle
- Independent Living Skills
- Emotional Adaptability
- Communication
- Social/Leisure Skills
- Community Integration
- Safety Awareness

Each ADP participant has her/his own individualized service plan (ISP) which is reviewed semiannually or annually with the interdisciplinary (ID) team (the consumer, parents/conservators, social worker, and FCSN staff). FCSN ADP operates from 8:45 a.m. to 2:45 p.m., Monday through Friday, year-round with a staff ratio of 1:3 or 1:4. Staff and students work hard together to build a full life and caring rapport with each other. "Miss Lena is like my boss," comments Cindy Anderson, an EBADP student, about her FCSN instructor. "She takes care of me and tells me how to be healthy, which is good." Caring for each other also means students reaching out to staff, to make them laugh, show compassion and empathy helping other students. "I [am] helping Karina with her seat belt," Renee Wu mentions proudly.

Come visit us to see how ADP participants spend their day and learn how the program has changed their lives. "I feel like I'm improving in many things – like reading, math...learning to be a better person and more social around people...I feel lucky to have a job at Walmart", says Cindy C. FCSN has helped ten students find a job at Walmart since 2006. This is a happy and energetic environment where participants enjoy learning and living through their daily activities.

## Living Services

FCSN currently operates two types of living services: Supported Living Services (SLS) and Independent Living Service (ILS) in Fremont and San Jose. Moving out of the family home for the first time can be overwhelming for both the consumer and his/ her parents. Our philosophy – "We Meet You Where You Are." FCSN Living Services are set to guide the participants through all aspects of living. SLS reviews the individualized service plan (ISP) quarterly with the interdisciplinary (ID) team. ILS reviews the ISP on a semi-annually or annually basis.

### *Supported Living Services (SLS)*

Participants live in a home of his/her choice, with 24/7 services and live-in staff if needed. FCSN SLS locates affordable housing in the community, finds roommate(s), and provides support and training to consumers.

### *Independent Living Services (ILS)*

FCSN provides two types of ILS:

a. Getting Ready

Intensive 1:1 ILS training is provided to consumers who are still residing with parents. The goal of this 2-year intensive training is to prepare them to move out of the family home either to live independently or in an SLS setting.

b.  Living Independently in the Community

For those who live independently in the community, FCSN ILS provides ongoing support and training to ensure the success of consumers' independent living arrangement. Our team provides individualized support and living skills training in the areas of:

- Self-care/Hygiene
- Balanced Meal Planning & Preparation
- Budgeting/Financial Responsibility
- Household Maintenance
- Optimal Health & Wellness
- Safety/Emergency Handling
- Social/Leisure Skills
- Community Integration

## Respite Services

FCSN values the power of families nurturing their children at home. However, family members need to take good care of themselves before they can provide care, supervision, and love to the disabled. If there is a need for parents to take a break, FCSN offers in-home respite services based on parents' requests and ensures that the disabled child or adult is supervised, assisted with self-care tasks when needed, and participates in his/her choice of activities at home.

FCSN Respite program offers varied schedules (seven days a week, flexible hours, minimum of 3-hour respite service each time) to meet families' needs.

FCSN is very blessed to have a pioneering board of directors guiding FCSN directions as well as many dedicated staff and volunteers contributing their intelligence, talents, love, and care to the special needs. We continue to make an effort to improve our staff and program quality, develop new programs, build a community for children and adults with special needs, and provide a village of support to them.

**East Bay Adult Day Program (EBADP) in 2014.**

# DREAM ACHIEVERS SENDS MESSAGE OF HOPE

## Anna Wang (Vice President of Local Programs), June 2014

Dream Achievers members. From left: Chris Koraltan, age 22, drummer/ percussionist; Lawrence Wang, age 24, saxophonist/flutist; Gregory Hebert, age 19, guitarist, Alice Jen, age 15, pianist.

**The Dream Achievers** is a music ensemble made up of talented young musicians with autism who have participated in Friends of Children with Special Needs (FCSN) music program. Founded two years ago, Dream Achievers members are Lawrence Wang, age 24, saxophonist/ flutist; Alice Jen, age 15, pianist; Gregory Hebert, age 19, guitarist; and Chris Koraltan, age 22, drummer/percussionist. Their repertoire includes over 120 songs that range from classical music to jazz/hip hop, Latin, kid-songs, and traditional cultural music. Due to autism, each one of the band members has an inspirational story of hope and amazing encouragement behind their music.

Even though Dream Achievers was formed two years ago, the ensemble has already performed in front of thousands and thousands of people. Some of the venues where they have performed include the California State Capitol, universities, convention centers, performing arts theaters, schools, companies, churches, and private events.

Last year, the band made a concert tour to Shanghai and Hong Kong. The entire trip was funded by a Chinese businessman and educator, Mr. Fang, who visited FCSN's music camp with his autistic son three years ago. Seeing the accomplishments of special needs children at FCSN, he returned home inspired and opened a school for children of day workers, denied enrollment in public schools, and included his son in the educational program.

In the Asian culture, shame and stigma can be associated with having a child with special needs. We traveled thousands of miles so people could see the talent of individuals with autism. The band became the ambassador of hope and a shining example that people with "disabilities" can have many special "abilities". The concerts touched people's hearts. Tears of hope and smiles of joy characterized the events. Special needs individuals gained encouragement to show everyone their own strength and abilities. The sponsors made videos of the concerts and the reaction of the audience to the beautiful music delivered by the Dream Achievers. Some of these videos are uploaded on YouTube. Search "Dream Achievers Concert of Hope" to locate them. The story of FCSN's pride and joy is still being written. These young people are going places and carrying out FCSN's mission: to give love, hope, respect, and support to the special needs community. For the past six months, the band has averaged more than one performance per week. Be sure to join Dream Achievers at their next concert or performance.

# SUPPORTED LIVING SERVICES

## Claire Brady (Supported Living Service Supervisor), Dec 2014

### *Learning and Growing While Having Fun*

For years, FCSN Supported Living Services (SLS) has been providing our consumers and their families support in important areas of their lives. We offer training and support in areas like living skills, socialization, and community integration. Some people have a misconception that SLS is all about training, household work, errands, etc. Some might not believe that SLS can also be about FUN and FUN-LEARNING. Please allow me to give a clearer picture of how much fun we have in SLS. This past year (2014), the FCSN SLS family had fun and educational activities and outings that our consumers and staffing team enjoyed. I personally think that we had too many activities to mention in one article, so I will trim it down to some of our bigger activities.

## Cooking Competition

Last October, FCSN SLS had a cooking contest. All of the apartments participated, and each apartment was asked to prepare a dish without any help from staff. All of our consumers did their best and won prizes in the end. This event allowed our consumers to showcase their talents and skills in the kitchen after years of training. The cooking competition was not only fun but it also taught everyone the value of teamwork. Thanks to the whole SLS support team, families, and especially Marie Cates for organizing this fun event!

Spring is usually the time for the majority of us to do a big cleaning in our homes. Our consumers do the same thing, and in the spring of 2014, a brilliant idea was brought up. Instead of throwing away, giving away, or storing things that owners do not need anymore, why not sell it for a very small price? So the Yard Sale plan was put together, thanks to our SLS parents especially Aunty Linmei. The Yard Sale was a huge success because not only did our consumers have much cleaner homes, they were also able to make some extra money. This event encouraged our consumers to go through their stuff and organize their belongings more efficiently.

## Art Class

Thanks to our very hardworking and selfless staff, friend, and case manager, Jenny, our consumers continue to enjoy going to a formal art class for free. A majority, if not all of our consumers, love art and find this activity very enjoyable. Consumers meet with Miss Jenny bi-weekly (two classes to accommodate all) and make very creative projects. These projects either end up being posted in their apartments, their parents' houses or sold for auction. Art class is a great example of fun learning because through this activity, our consumers learn the value of discipline and following instructions.

This past year, the SLS group has gone to very fun and educational field trips. Aside from the usual parks and malls, big trips were scheduled for our consumers which were always well attended. In FCSN SLS, we value our consumers' inputs so we leave it up to them to decide where they want to go. A planning committee (consisting of all our consumers) meeting is scheduled every three months to discuss activities that they want to do. Depending on the outcome of the meeting, our SLS management team works on scheduling the trips or activities. Some of the trips we had were to Great America, Monterey Bay Aquarium, Academy of Sciences, Alameda County Fair, etc.

## Our Team

Our SLS family will not be as complete, happy, and successful without our devoted "direct support staff, trainers, or life coaches." Through their hard work and dedication, we are able to serve and provide support to our consumers and their families. A very big thank you is in order, so THANK YOU TO EVERYONE IN OUR SLS TEAM! Seeing all of our consumers' growth and progress makes me so proud to be part of SLS and, of course, FCSN. We had some challenges in 2014, but through everyone's (parents, Sylvia, accounting, and HR) support and guidance, we finished the year right. I am excited to see what 2015 has in store for us.

# SPECIAL NEEDS GOT TALENT 2015

## Anna Wang (Vice President of Local Programs), Dec 2014

### *Discovering Talent in Unexpected Places*

You've heard of America's Got Talent and American Idol? Get ready for the latest in talent show competition, Special Needs Got Talent (SNGT) – Discovering Talent in Unexpected Places, presented by Friends of Children with Special Needs (FCSN) and proudly sponsored by Everybody is a Star and the Golden State Warriors.

SNGT is currently recruiting adults and children from across California with developmental disabilities to showcase their talents. All types of performances are welcomed: musical acts, dancing, comedy, magic acts, martial arts, acrobatics, etc. Participation medals will be awarded to every contestant. Trophies and prizes will be awarded to all finalists at the Final Competition. All individuals with developmental disabilities are encouraged to try out and have the chance to enjoy an extraordinary experience!

Only 70 applicants will be accepted, and already more than 50 applicants have signed up to perform at the preliminary auditions. The Preliminary Auditions will be held on Feb. 8 at 1 p.m. at the Friends of Children with Special Needs Dream Center, 2300 Peralta Boulevard, Fremont, CA 94536. The final competition will be held March 14 at 7 p.m. at the Santa Clara Convention Center at 5001 Great America

Parkway, Santa Clara. Application deadline is January 31. From preliminary auditions, judges will whittle contestants down to 12 finalists, who will receive $100 in prize money. The top three winners will each receive a $500 cash prize and a recording session and a broadcast quality promotional video, valued at $18,000, to submit to talent scouts, thanks to our sponsor, Everybody is a Star, Judges include Grammy and Golden Globes Award winning composer and performer, Kitaro; composer and worldwide performing pianist, Stephen Prutsman; as well as, other celebrity judges to be named. Other judges include the honorable Senator Jim Beall; Assembly member Kansen Chu; Executive Director of California's Department of Developmental Services Santi Rogers; Executive Director of the Regional Center of the East Bay Jim Burton; Executive Director of the San Andreas Regional Center Javier Zaldivar, and founder of California Line Dance Association of America Kico Lin.

"This event is already attracting national attention," says lead organizer, Auntie Anna, vice president of Local Programs and Community Relations and cofounder of FCSN, an organization begun in 1996 by ten Chinese American families. Today the organization To Dream the Impossible Dream 13 has grown to serve more than 800 multi-ethnic families with children and adults with special needs through multiple programs in the East Bay and South Bay. FCSN has garnered a number of awards, most recently as "Provider of the Year," presented by the San Andrea Regional Center serving Monterey, San Benito, Santa Clara and Santa Cruz Counties.

"This is a great opportunity for some people to jumpstart a career of the very talented and create a goal that everyone in our community can strive for," continued Auntie Anna, who envisions the event as an opportunity for developmentally disabled people to showcase talent.

Employment rates for developmentally disabled people, she notes, are "pathetically low" due to stereotypes.

FCSN is well-known for dreaming big so expect this first year of the event to become the launch pad for a national Special Needs Got Talent in future years. "Actually, I think this can grow to become a world event like the Special Olympics," says Auntie Anna. FCSN is in contact with television producers, hoping to convince them to create a reality series to showcase the raw talent "that may be a little awkward, but genuine, and not yet commercialized. I think American viewers are ready and interested in performers who are a little less packaged, but remarkable and marketable," added Auntie Anna.

Auntie Anna is passionate about this event, in part, because of her own experience with her son, Lawrence, now age 25 and an accomplished saxophone soloist and vocalist in FCSN's Dream Achievers band. Lawrence and other band members are autistic.

From a young age, Lawrence was afraid of sound and music. He covered his ears, ran away, and called out, "Stop! Stop! Stop!"

"Naturally, music was adverse to him. I didn't know at the time that he was having a sensory overload reaction," recalls Auntie Anna.

During one of the FCSN summer musical camps, an instructor taught the simple instrument, the recorder. At the end of the four days, she asked students to play. When no one volunteered, she called on Lawrence, who again had sat in the corner each day with his back to the class and his ears covered. To everyone's amazement, Lawrence stood, played each song perfectly and sat down.

The teacher offered Lawrence free flute lessons. Auntie Anna recalls, "I didn't have to pay the flute teacher, but I had to pay Lawrence to go. He hated the high-pitch 'noise' of the flute." Two months later, he was playing as a soloist in a flute ensemble. He joined a band. Drowned out by electrical guitars and drums, Lawrence was asked by the band leader to play a louder instrument. That's when Lawrence turned to the saxophone. A month later, he was playing any tune on the radio.

"It was a miracle to discover that Lawrence had musical talent that now gives him immense pleasure. He's performing every week. His friends are the band members. He has purpose," says Auntie Anna, "and a way to contribute to society. How many more talents are out there with the talent still in them because developmental disability is so misunderstood?"

# BUILDING FCSN'S SOUTH BAY CENTER

## James Chiao (President 2014-2015), June 2015

**South Bay Center design team in 2014.**

## South Bay Center Construction

It is great news that our South Bay Center construction is underway. After a long wait, we finally received the city's building permit in early April 2015. Within days, the construction company, ACON, completed the demolition of the building interiors. Then suddenly we were ready for the renovation phase. Demolition and total interior renovation are necessary to meet the design requirements of our South Bay programs. By the time we finish, we will have a brand-new facility with classrooms, kitchen, multi-purpose room, offices, computer room, workshop, and a cafe/store – all customized to meet our current and future needs.

## South Bay Center Teams

The South Bay Center renovation project is a huge undertaking for our organization. Fortunately, FCSN gained some experience building the Dream Project in Fremont. To help direct the effort, we have formed many teams: a design team, a construction team, a store team, an IT team, and more recently, an interior design team. Over the past six months, working with the architect, the design team has finalized the floor plan. The construction team, under David Tu, Stanley Woo, and Albert Wong, is now monitoring costs as well as construction progress, with regular on-site meetings. The store team has been working on cafe/store layout, the menu, and equipment list.

Our IT team has been busy defining the requirements for network connections, wireless routers, and telephones. Our interior design team also started a few weeks ago, with help from Mandy Chang, a professional interior designer from MGI Interior Design. Other help came in unexpected ways. For example, through board member Jason Wong, we have received some donated office furniture.

We are especially proud that many South Bay parents have joined our teams. It is with their involvement that we can ensure the success of local programs and the South Bay Center as a community center.

## First "Special Needs Got Talent"

Back in 2002, FCSN organized our first Chinese folk song concert at the Santa Clara Convention Center Theater, an event that was hugely popular in the Bay Area's Chinese community. Late last year, we considered repeating the feat by organizing another event at exactly the same location. The goal was to publicize our South Bay Center project, to involve special needs families, and to reach out to new audiences. FCSN Vice President Anna Wang came up with the idea of expanding FCSN's talent show, and "Special Needs Got Talent" was born. Soon, we attracted the attention of another non-profit organization, "Everybody Is A Star" foundation, whose founder, Howard Sapper, brought in the Golden State Warriors and San Francisco Giants as sponsors. We also lined up several key people in our community as judges.

For the February 2015 audition, we had judges with impressive credentials: Howie Morris, ten times judge for the Grammy Award; Jinye Wang, founder of Artch Inc, and board member of California Music Teachers Association; and Jim Burton, Executive Director of Regional Center of the East Bay.

For the final performance and competition at the Santa Clara Convention Center, we had another impressive list of judges, with renowned musician and composer Kitaro, a Grammy and Golden Globe Award winner, heading the list that included: Mimi Kwan, ABC7 TV Vice President of Community Affairs; Jim Beall, Honorable Senator; Kansen Chu, Assembly Member; and Santi Rogers, Executive Director of Calif. State Department of Developmental Services,

News about our event spread to many special needs communities throughout Northern California. More than seventy entries, with some teams coming from as far away as Sacramento, auditioned in February. The final performance on March 14th was a huge success. We had a variety of performances from comedy, dance, singing to musical instruments, all performed by special needs individuals from different ethnic groups. Many of us have attended "special performances" before, but this one was an eye opener. It swept the audience off their feet. The event achieved all the objectives we set and far exceeded our expectations. With this kind of success, we have pretty much ensured the continuation of this event next year.

## Looking forward

It is hard to believe that our first staff joined FCSN in 2005. This year, for the first time, we have begun to recognize our staff with more than five years of service to FCSN. In addition, we also want to recognize our volunteers, many of whom have been with FCSN for more than fifteen years. We truly appreciate their dedication, their passion, and their commitment to further our mission and cause.

With the start of construction of the South Bay Center, FCSN is on the way to build another Dream Center, this time in San Jose; we expect completion by the fourth quarter of this year. However, with the rising cost of real estate properties and construction, the cost of the South Bay Center now totals $4 million. Our original budget of $2.5 million for the South Bay Center project looks very much inadequate. We are counting on raising $1.5M to help with the project. Last year, with the huge support from our members, friends, and supporters, we raised over $600K. We are setting a goal of $500K for this year to close the gap between the budgeted and the actual cost.

FCSN has come a long way since the humble beginning in 1996. By the time we open the South Bay Center, we can further expand our programs and provide more support to the families in Santa Clara County. This is another big step in our journey to build a community and deliver happiness to special needs families and others in our community.

**Interior of South Bay Center after demolition in 2015.**

# FCSN STAFF APPRECIATION EVENT

Nayeli Toto (Supported Living Services Manager), June 2015

## *A BIG Family We Are*

FCSN Staff Appreciation has become one of my favorite events throughout the years. It is a very special day for staff from all departments to join together and celebrate one more year of hard work, dedication, and service to our consumers. In anticipation of this celebration, I experienced an overwhelming feeling of gratitude to those who come to work every day with a positive attitude, willingness to help and an open heart.

This year, our celebration was particularly unique due to the great turnout and the joie de vivre we all could feel. Employees from all departments, the management team and board members gathered in the FCSN multipurpose room for a cohesive and refreshing get-together. Participants have provided their feedback about how much they enjoyed the games the management team prepared this year, including the "Balloon Shaving" event, in which partners competed in teamwork and communication by "shaving" balloons while one partner was blindfolded, and the "FCSN Trivia Game," which tested teams of participants on their knowledge of random facts about FCSN's operations and management team. Another highlight of the day was the raffle: everyone who attended was given a raffle ticket, and names were later drawn from the raffle box to be matched with amazing prizes. I appreciated FCSN Board of Directors who donated many valuable prizes so that every participant took a prize home this year. I saw many excited, cheerful and thankful faces across the room; it was overall a very successful event.

This important Staff Appreciation event was absolutely not an exception to our usual teamwork in making preparations and arrangements. All departments did their part. Sylvia came early in the morning to cook prime rib for lunch; Vivian prepared breakfast and even volunteered her husband, Chris, to make delicious porridge and vegetables for everyone; Kathy (ADP teacher) made delicious scones and cookies; and the SLS CM team prepared fruit. From setting the room, to preparing drinks and fruit, to the final clean up, everyone offered a helping hand even though this was a celebration for all of us.

I am thankful for such an amazing event and also for the hard work, dedication and willing hearts that everyone brings to the FCSN team.

# 2015 SPECIAL NEEDS GOT TALENT SHOW

## Kenneth Song (FCSN Dream Builders Reporter), June 2015

**David Ren, the harpist.**

Why do we enjoy the sound of music? Why do we like to dance? These trivial combinations of sounds and movements of the body resonate deeply with some primal aspect of human emotion. Perhaps they are ancient artifacts of human imagination, reminding us to rejoice in the very act of being alive, flexing the muscles and vocal chords we were designed to have. But music can also stir feelings of sorrow in our breast. Dance can also be solemn and introspective. Indeed, it is difficult – daresay impossible – to put into words why we love to sing and dance, but I believe that there is one group of special individuals who have come closer to understanding the truth than the rest of us. For socially handicapped individuals, these talents are outlets for a train of convoluted thoughts and emotions they might otherwise not be able to express. I was powerfully reminded of this through my experience at the 2015 Special Needs Got Talent show.

As the lights in the theatre dimmed and the bustle of conversation hushed to a low murmur, I found it hard to believe how far these talented young students of FCSN had come in the span of a single year. I had seen many of these same young individuals perform in March 2014 at the FCSN headquarters in Fremont; the sheer upscale of the preparations that had gone into this year's talent show had me feeling excited before the curtains even opened. Dressed in classy attire, more than 600 people packed into the beautifully set theatre at the Santa Clara Convention Center. From a preliminary pool of seventy performers and groups from all across California, twelve finalists were chosen to compete in the final round of Special Needs Got Talent. Among the esteemed judges were Kitaro, a Golden Globe-winning producer and composer of new age music; Mimi Kwan, a vice president from ABC7 television channel; Senator Jim Beall; Assembly member Kansen Chu; and Santi J. Rogers, California State Director of the Department of Developmental Services. I was given the special privilege of going backstage before the show to capture the atmosphere of excitement among the performers.

Comedian Loren Moale was bubbling with excitement as he prepared to give the opening performance. Loren had traveled from Napa with his family so he could represent Everybody Is A Star Foundation, headquartered in Sonoma. Firmly grasping my hand, he startled me with his confidence but was happy to share all about his work as an announcer on several local radio stations. Loren's love of theatre and performance stems from his early experiences acting in a variety of plays at school, and his acting skills certainly showed as he commanded the stage alongside the master of ceremonies, ABC7 Television Reporter Matt Keller as they kicked off the show. Loren's dedication to the art of communication has given him a niche in society and certainly promises to further build his inspiring career in the future. Toward the start of the talent show, the audience was treated to a music video, sponsored by the Everybody Is A Star Foundation, starring Loren himself in "I Just Haven't Met You Yet." The production quality and Loren's performance were superb, reminding the audience that SNGT winners would also receive their own high quality music videos produced. What Loren has managed to accomplish so far in his young life with the support of his family and friends is truly amazing and sheds a beacon for special needs individuals everywhere.

I also spoke with instrumentalist ChiLing Wu, whose mother shared that he had hummed along to every audible song even before he was able to speak at the age four due to autism. Luckily, his parents were quick to identify a hidden reserve of talent ChiLing had for music, and they could see the joy and purpose that music brings to his life. Extremely soft-spoken, ChiLing makes a statement with his proficiency on piano, drums, cello, dulcimer, and saxophone; he regularly entertains as a pianist for Kaiser Permanente. Here is a shining example of how individuals with special needs can be nurtured into productive and valuable members of society. I can only imagine what comfort and companionship music and playing his instruments have brought to this 24-year-old prodigy as he deals with what can be a complicated and confusing world. Last year, ChiLing won a silver medal at the 2013 International Piano Festival for People with Disabilities in Vienna, a testament to his musical talents.

During the talent show, the audience was shown a video that gave an inside look at competitors and their incredible journeys during the preliminary rounds. When asked by the interviewers, many special needs performers had difficulties answering how much they practiced or describing what they planned to perform. They either struggled to comprehend the questions or were too shy to give an exact response. However, in the simplest yet most beautiful words I could imagine, several captured the profound significance that music and dance holds for them. One young boy stated boldly: "Music has the soul inside of me." Another girl whispered to the camera, as if a precious secret, "Dancing has the energy to help me be cured." These short statements touched me. I quickly began to understand how these talented young individuals continued to improve so dramatically from year to year. They instinctively understood that music and dance hold the power to break down linguistic and social barriers that surround them. They were deeply in love with the talents they could perform as a means of truly expressing themselves to the rest of the world.

Each of the twelve finalists had something unique and exciting to offer the audience that night. The Magic Makers band with Tony Salazar on the keyboard, Andrew Wilson on the drums, and ChiLing Wu on the bass opened with a lively cultural performance of "La Bamba." Alice Jen enchanted with a piano lullaby *Autumn Moon on a Clear Lake* and 13-year-old William Dong impressed with a classical piano performance of a Mozart sonata. Dream Seekers' *Gentleman* and Resplandor Folklorico's *Jarabe Tapatio Corta* treated the audience to dances. The latter was a real cultural treat as young performers were garbed in authentic Mexican folk dance costumes–males tap dancing and females twirling their dresses. Bernard Smith swept the theatre with his voice and piano performance of *They Can't Take that Away from Me*. Greg Hebert and Michael Valcour rocked out on guitars, their deep voices set to the melodies of *Take Me Home, Country Roads* and *I Can See Clearly Now*. Several more unique instrumentalists performed that night: Lawrence Wang with a saxophone rendition of *Desafinido* and David Ren with a soothing harp version of *Over the Rainbow*. To round off the night, Jasmine Dana executed a well-timed choreography to a Bollywood dance in a mesmerizing white, green, and orange dress. The Dream Achievers band consisting of Lawrence, Alice, and Greg hit the last sweet note with their performance of *Rude* with full instrumentation and vocals by the young, talented group of three.

At the end of the night, the three top performances selected by the judges were David Ren with his magnificent solo harp rendition, the Magic Makers band, and the Dream Achievers band. All the participating groups and individuals involved went home with a trophy and a prize, so in the true spirit of the FCSN event, everyone involved was a winner. I continue to be impressed by the quality of care and instruction that FCSN provides to its students. Only one year ago, I was amazed by the incredible talent of these young individuals, and I will testify that their talents continue to grow exponentially with each passing year. I even unearthed something within myself at this year's annual talent show: a deeper appreciation for the power of music and dance.

# LOOKING BACK AND LOOKING FORWARD

## Yee-Yeen Wang (President 2015-2016), Dec 2015

Six months ago, I was elected by the FCSN board to serve as president. Looking back, over the past nine years, under previous presidents Tsai-Wei Wu, Jim Chiao, and the management team, I see that FCSN has established a firm foundation for the organization, which prepared us for another growth phase. First of all, after years of site search, we purchased the Bascom property in April 2014 and construction started in April 2015. We expect to complete the renovation project by the end of the first quarter 2016 and open the South Bay Center in the second quarter of 2016. Modelled after the Dream Center in Fremont, this Dream Project is our second building creating a community center to provide more complete services for our South Bay families. We thank all of our members, friends, and donors for their numerous contributions and generous support.

In 2015, FCSN continued development of many enrichment programs. Through various local programs, we have helped many special needs individuals to learn and grow in a friendly and supportive environment. All these accomplishments are possible because of the devotion of many of our parents and volunteers. FCSN has received numerous awards for our Adult Day Programs, our Supported Living Service, and for our community services. These awards are a reflection of the quality of service and dedication of our staff and parents.

Looking forward to 2016, FCSN will soon start its 20th year. We have come a long way, but there still is a lot of work for us to do to move ahead. Most of all, we need to complete the South Bay Center construction on time; this is paramount for us to open the center in the second quarter of 2016. Secondly, we will continue to expand our services and improve the service quality to fulfill our members' needs. Last but not the least, given our limited resources, the FCSN board has set an objective to look for opportunities to improve our operating efficiency.

Based upon our beliefs and values, FCSN has the goal to help special needs children and their families, creating a community where we offer love, hope, and respect in a supportive environment. It is also our job in 2016 to bring members closer to each other and closer with the surrounding communities.

FCSN is a big family. The founding families had nothing but a belief when they started the organization in 1996. Today, many of us are reaping the benefit as part of this big family. As FCSN celebrates its 20th year, we will continue moving forward based on the same belief and mission.

With all of us working together, we will create a better tomorrow for our children and families.

# WAKE-UP CALL: ADVOCACY NEEDED NOW

## Johnna Laird (FCSN Dream Builders Reporter), Dec 2015

*An Interview with Anna Wang*

Supporters of increased funding for people with special needs rallied on the steps of the State Capitol following Governor Jerry Brown's release of the California State Budget in January.

Were you there?

In the thirteen years since Anna Wang, FCSN's Vice President of Enrichment Programs and Community Relations, has considered herself an advocate for people with developmental disabilities, she says she has seen less involvement by parents in the political process and as a result, less commitment by legislators. "Legislators and parents alike have grown numb to the issues facing people within the developmental disabilities community," says Anna.

"There is less engagement by parents, which is the opposite of what happened when five parents refused to leave the State Capitol until they were guaranteed passage of the Lanterman Act," Anna explains.

Anna thinks complacency may partly be due to age. "Parents today weren't around to remember when people with developmental disabilities were housed like animals in institutions," she says.

The Lanterman Act, first passed in 1969, followed by subsequent related legislation, changed that. The Lanterman Act guaranteed people with developmental disabilities the right to get services and support they need to live in the community like people without disabilities. "The spirit of the Lanterman Act started when a handful of parents went to Sacramento to advocate for their children. Parents didn't like the living situations their children were in and wanted a better life for them. Those parents won rights and benefits for all people with special needs, not just their own children.

Now it's the law that the state of California has responsibility to take care and support the lives of people with developmental disabilities so they can live in the community and have a real life," Anna explains.

Instead of seeing the global picture of eroding services, parents often take the Lanterman law for granted, says Anna, while state officials keep trimming back funds, refusing to grant raises for more than a decade. This makes it difficult for organizations that provide services through the Regional Centers to operate. Locally and statewide, more than one third of programs have closed while the special needs population has doubled. (That's two-thirds of the providers giving services to a population that's 200 percent of what it was ten years ago.) Gone are Lynn Center in Contra Costa County that served more than 500 preschoolers with special needs, Harambee Kinship Center in Hayward that served special needs adults with severe behavioral challenges, and CARH in Castro Valley that served the special needs community for 42 years.

"It's apparent when we see legislators getting less and less sensitive to the needs and the sense of urgency that the entire support system is collapsing, that parents need to get involved." she says

"It is the government's responsibility, but the government can change. Parents can become too dependent on the government. There's still a lot we as parents can do within our families to enrich and make a fulfilling life for our special needs loved ones. There is low-hanging fruit that could be picked to help our children.

"When governmental services collapse, I don't think we will know what to do. This is disheartening to see, especially here in Silicon

Valley where there is so much brain power and so many resources. Not every parent feels powerful, but when parents team up together as a group they can move mountains like the pioneering parents of the Lanterman Act. Together, parents become powerful advocates. Ours is a government 'of the people, by the people and for the people,'" says Anna. Without parents putting pressure on legislators, the situation facing people with developmental disabilities looks grim, she adds.

"Legislators are ignoring people with special needs. We don't have dedicated lobbyists like other industries. We have an advocacy problem."

What are the first steps Anna suggests parents take? "For the future of our loved ones, families need to be relentless. We need to persist, so the Lanterman Act does not go away. Going to Sacramento might be difficult for many of us, but visiting our State legislators' at their local office to voice our concerns is just as effective. At the same time, we parents can't put all our eggs into the Lanterman basket. We need to plan our own children's future. Our children need places to live. They need employment and interests to help them live more fulfilled lives. We are the voices to secure their future. We have to facilitate the future now so it will be on autopilot when we are gone. Be sure to join us at the next FCSN Dream Project meeting. Now is the time. It's our call to action."

# DRAMA CAMP: WHO WANTS TO BE A STAR

Johnna M. Laird (FCSN Dream Builders Reporter), Dec 2015

Plans are already in the works for the fifth annual FCSN Drama Camp.

Shh! Don't tell anyone, but camp leaders may have narrowed play choices to *Despicable Me* or *Madagascar.*

The fourth annual camp presentation, *Toy Story,* in August 2015, drew more than 30 special needs students to act on stage, plus 27 youth and 15 adult volunteers. A packed audience attended the evening performance at New Hope Church Community Church, next door to the FCSN Dream Center in Fremont. Dancers from the event performed again on stage at FCSN's Gala in October.

21 year old Kelsey Findlay made her directing debut with *Toy Story.* A veteran of the theater, Kelsey has a stack of playbills from her

performances in school and with Star Struck Theater, most recently as Ursula in this winter's production of *The Little Mermaid*.

Previous Drama Camp productions have included *The Lion King* (2012), *The Wizard of Oz* (2013), and *Finding Nemo* (2014).

For anyone not yet caught in the excitement of a three-day camp (translate that to less than eight hours of rehearsals) with production on the fourth day, videos are available on YouTube.

Plan to attend either *Despicable Me* or *Madagascar* this August. The price is right – tickets are free.

# AN INTERVIEW WITH FCSN'S EXECUTIVE BUSINESS DIRECTOR

Johnna M. Laird (FCSN Dream Builders Reporter), June 2016

In the ten years since the Peralta Dream Center opened to its first seven consumers, FCSN has grown to serve approximately 200 adult consumers in its Living Services, Respite, and Adult Day Programs in Fremont and San Jose. Additionally, through afterschool programs, sports, summer camps, therapeutic programs, support groups and family seminars, FCSN serves 300 families with special needs on a regular basis and has more than 1,000 families in its membership.

In this past decade, FCSN has garnered awards, earned stellar reviews from consumers and families, and developed a prospective consumer wait list that extends for years. FCSN founders laid the planks of success with their vision, captured in the mission statement that guides the organization.

What makes FCSN successful? Executive Business Director Sylvia Yeh resoundingly credits FCSN's employees, "our devoted staff," for FCSN's reputation and high-caliber experience that consumers and families receive.

"Our staff members are very, very devoted. Their contributions and dedication have made differences in the consumers' lives they serve," says Sylvia. She explains that her management team looks for people who "have the heart" for working with consumers. "Experience is important, but we can train. We provide training to our staff on a regular basis. The people we hire must have the mindset and want to work with this population. We focus on what consumers can do, instead of what they can't. We are here to help them live out their potential and shine."

As a key to its workforce, FCSN seeks and attracts young, mature, energetic, and educated adults, most of whom hold bachelor's degrees, as a key to its workforce. This energy and enthusiasm empower staff to design creative curriculum to motivate consumers in their learning. FCSN focuses on person-centered services and operates from the consumer's viewpoint. FCSN currently has 100+ employees.

"Due to limited funding from DDS, our jobs are not high-paid, especially for the Bay Area," says Sylvia, "so the staff that work at FCSN find the work rewarding through the relationships they build with this by population they serve and by expressing their creativity to empower consumers. "I just cannot say thanks enough. The number one reason we have the program that we do is because of our people, our staff. They are the people who deserve the thanks."

Sylvia also indicates another element that distinguishes FCSN from other programs is the Individual Service Plan report, generated by the staff and coordinator on a semi-annual and annual basis. The response from parents is overwhelmingly positive, says Sylvia. As an example, she remembered a recent comment from parent Kim Bostrom who received a report after her daughter's first 30 days at FCSN.

"I just want to thank you for all the time you put in to creating that 30-day report about my daughter's progress. I have NEVER seen anything so professional in her whole life full of reports, and there have been many, as you might imagine. For the first time ever, I feel as if my daughter is in a place where she can really grow and develop: where she is being actively ENCOURAGED and HELPED to learn new things, by loving and devoted staff. I cannot express the degree of relief and thankfulness this brings me. "Kim says she maintained her daughter on the wait list for six years because FCSN has impressed her with FCSN's programs.

FCSN ADP staff members also make a video or DVD for each consumer's annual review. The film captures the consumer's daily activities, training, socialization, and participation at FCSN. Consumers seem as delighted as parents, seeing and sharing the videos. Parents whose children participate in the Supported Living Program appreciate weekly communication reports to know how their adult children spend their time at FCSN, in which activities they participate, their health conditions, and the challenges they encounter in the week.

Sylvia started her employment with FCSN in May 2006 as the second FCSN employee. She brought with her 10 years of regional center experience. Clearly understanding the FCSN vision, Sylvia designed the adult day program and living services to include socialization, communication, academic and living skills, fun, and community involvement. The first seven consumers started in fall 2006.

"It took us two years to build our reputation," says Sylvia, "and by 2008 we were getting tons of referrals." Both East Bay Adult Day Program (EBADP) and Supported Living Services reached its capacity. To serve more consumers, Sylvia designed another adult day program – Community Integrated Day Program (CIDP) and secured vendorization from the Regional Center of East Bay in 2009. Within a year and half, CIDP reached its capacity of 48 consumers. The South Bay program, headed by Vivian Chung, currently serves 44 consumers. With a new South Bay Center opening in the next few months, FCSN hopes to expand capacity to better serve the San Jose area.

Sylvia also applied for and obtained Caltrans grants in 2012. FCSN received two mid-size buses in August 2015. In January 2016, FCSN transportation service was vendored by Regional Center of East Bay. Currently the bus transports 23 consumers to and from the program on a daily basis as well as transports consumers to vocational training sites and field trip destinations. Transportation is expected to continue to expand. Sylvia submitted another grant application to Caltrans in 2014. FCSN expects to receive two more vans in mid-2017. In 2016, FCSN is targeting growth of its Independent Living Service (ILS) Program as well as developing more job opportunities and volunteer work for its participants.

"As FCSN reaches this 20th anniversary milestone, the FCSN management team and staff are committed to continue to provide quality services to consumers and their families," says Sylvia. "Building a brighter future for special needs individuals is the ultimate goal of FCSN."

# CREATING A BRIGHTER FUTURE

## Yee-Yeen Wang (President 2015-2016), June 2016

**We celebrated FCSN's 20th anniversary at our annual meeting & family day in 2016.**

FCSN has entered its 20th year. It is an incredible feat for a non-profit organization to grow from ten families to today's more than 1000 family members and 100 staff.

### The Constants: FCSN's Mission and Visions

The force behind our growth arose from setting a clear mission and vision from the very beginning: we want to help children with special needs and their families, and to build a community for them. Because of this simple yet consistent message, it was easy for the members, staff, and friends to bond together and to receive support from the community. I believe FCSN will grow over the next ten or twenty years under the same philosophy.

In the past, we have often heard at FCSN that "we are not here to provide you with fish, but to teach you how to fish." Many of our programs are based on the needs observed by the parents, designed by the parents, and organized by the parents; such programs help our own kids and other individuals alike. We can think of FCSN as a platform, where parents can gather together, design and develop the necessary programs and services. After twenty years of growth, FCSN has gained more experience and ability to help parents. However, at the same time, we are concerned about losing that entrepreneurship or drive due to preoccupation with service programs in the market.

## The Changes – New Way of Thinking and Service Content

Over the past ten years, both in concept and in practice, FCSN has developed many new ideas and techniques for our educational and training programs. In the decade ahead, FCSN will continue to encourage our parents and staff to try new ideas and methods to help our children and adults.

The widespread use of the Internet and social media has changed the way we communicate with others. FCSN will expand our use of the new technologies to bring us together, to share our needs and experiences, and to allow better understanding by others in our community.

## Together, let's build a brighter future

People are at the heart of our organization. To have FCSN as a platform in the long run, we need to involve more, younger families. Our care of individuals of all ages with special needs will provide new challenges for FCSN as our adult population advances in years. We also need to take care of our staff, because they are the force who bring our wishes into reality.

In 2006, the completion of the FCSN Center in Fremont marked a key milestone for the first Dream Project and the beginning of services in the East Bay. Ten years later, in 2016, we have just witnessed the completion of the FCSN South Bay Center in San Jose. This milestone also marks the beginning of phase two of the second Dream Project to provide more services in the South Bay.

Members, staff, and friends: let's continue working together for the next ten years to continue to create a community of love, hope, respect, and support for our special children. Thank you.

# WEAVING OUR DREAM

Johnna M. Laird (FCSN Dream Builders Reporter & Parent),
Dec 2016

*A Successful 2016 FCSN Fundraising Gala*

**FCSN Co-Ed group dancing in front of a colorful backdrop at FCSN annual
fundraising gala "Weaving Our Dream". (2016)**

FCSN's 20th Anniversary Weaving Our Dream Fundraising Gala
attracted more than 1,000 people from throughout the San Francisco
Bay Area. A celebratory evening of dinner, entertainment, and dancing
on November 5, 2016, at the Convention Center in Santa Clara raised
more than $400,000, vital for FCSN programs.

Performers from FCSN's Fremont and South Bay programs
moved into the limelight with a glistening backdrop and became
the highlight of the evening. Their performances followed a rousing
fundraiser as attendees lifted numbered programs, offering donations
ranging from tens of thousands to hundreds of dollars. This year's

fundraiser brought in technology, allowing donations via smart phones to send the goal-setting thermometer on stage rising.

South Bay Adult Day Program performed *Take the Samba Train*; Summer Music Camp Band played *We Are the World*; Summer Drama Camp gyrated to a Madagascar Dance Medley; the Co-ed Dance Zumba and Line Group's moved to *Most Dazzling Folk Style*; Dream Seekers Dance Team sang *I Want It That Way* and kicked up their heels to *Can't Stop the Feeling*; and Chinese Music Ensemble's *Tumbling Walnuts* left the audience shaking their heads in amazement.

FCSN's Dream Achievers Band, which performs regularly in the San Francisco Bay Area, accompanied Hollywood's Chris Showerman, known for his roles in Disney's George of the Jungle 2, television's Supergirl, and Radio America, a production he wrote and directed. Chris sang *Wind Beneath My Wings* and *Impossible Dream*. The band returned at the end of the evening to close the night and get attendees on their feet dancing.

Chris Showerman also chose to debut an original song he wrote with the artist SEAL in mind. Chris performed *Anyway* because it fit FCSN's "inspiring theme...and the spirit of FCSN." "All Things Possible" is Chris's motto; Chris noted the verses address fears and stories "we tell ourselves that stifle action toward our dream." The chorus reminds: "Do It Anyway."

A number of state and regional dignitaries attended the event that began as guests arrived in flowing gowns and dark suits to first peruse dozens of raffle and auction prizes before entering the banquet hall for dinner. Raffle prizes ranged from an iPhone 7 to a trip for four to Disneyland to baskets with gift cards, and auction prizes of a five-day ocean resort stay in Cancun to box seats for a Golden State Warriors game, donated by Alameda County Supervisor Scott Haggerty.

ABC7-TV General Assignment Reporter Matt Keller, emcee for the evening who has also emceed FCSN's Special Needs Talent Showcase, kept the evening lively with heartfelt and witty remarks.

Usually seen as a master of ceremonies, Dr. Albert Wang, an FCSN founder and Chairman of the Board of Palo Alto Medical Foundation, provided a different perspective, telling a parent's story of how FCSN has changed his and his family's lives (see Parent Sharing article).

Crystal awards were handed out by FCSN Board Chairman Professor Chenming Hu and FCSN President Yee-Yee Wang to long-time supporters of FCSN, who provided help to the organization's pioneers as they took steps to transform a vision into reality. Those recognized included: China Airlines, Eva Airlines, New York Life Insurance Company, ASI Corp., Bizlink Technology, Inc., ClubSport, Henkel Corporation, Mission Peak Homes, Palo Alto Medical Foundation, J & V Foundation, and Kaiser Permanente. T. J. Maxx and Walmart were also recognized as corporations that have hired and continue to employ FCSN consumers. In addition, individuals receiving crystal awards for longtime support included: Sandy and Ruth Chau, CC and Regina Yin, E. Wang and R. Busher, Chenming and Margaret Hu, Limin Hu, Albert and Anna Wang, Jim and Linmei Chiao, CC Shih, LS and RT Huang Foundation.

"I look forward to this event every year, joining this community for an evening of entertainment, inspiration and togetherness," remarked special education teacher Lisa Hillman of Glankler School in Fremont afterward.

California State Assembly Assistant Majority Whip Evan Low described the evening as celebrating FCSN's "unwavering dedication to building a strong, caring, and respectful community for individuals with special needs."

He commended FCSN for its "years of hard work" and applauded its "success over the past two decades." He thanked FCSN for promoting "values of love, hope and respect in our community."

Crystal Awards for many long-time supporters of FCSN.

# A TRIP YOU DON'T WANT TO MISS

## Roxana Chiu (FCSN parent), Dec 2016

### *FCSN Families Explore California*

**Santa Cruz Roaring Camp Train Ride.**

The tradition of the FCSN biannual family bus trip started four years ago. Many of our children loved to go on trips with their friends and families; therefore, we started this family bus trip activity to allow our families the opportunity to enjoy a fun day in a relaxing setting.

Our bus trips cover many different activities including: ferries, trains, and boat rides, national parks, and museums. We have travelled to Carmel, Napa, Santa Cruz, Monterey, Sausalito, Tiburon, and many other exciting locations. To accommodate families from the East Bay and South Bay, we offer two pick up/drop off sites for our families. Families enjoy a hot breakfast in the bus while we drive to our first destination. Most trips will include up to three destinations with a three-hour lunch break so that families can take some time to explore the town and get lunch based on their own preferences. We always include lots of walking activity in our trips since our children have a strong motivation to walk longer when they travel with their peers. Walking through these beautiful, natural settings is a main reason for the bus trip.

As our children love the bus trip dearly, it almost seems that twice a year seems not enough for the occasion. Many families over the years have asked for additional trips; therefore, we added a Walking Around Town program this year to meet that request. The purpose of Walking Around Town is to explore different towns by taking public transportation like Caltrain or BART. Walking Around Town offers a less stressful, shorter trip that everyone can enjoy. Families can join the group on trip day by meeting with everyone at the Caltrain station. Walking Around Town usually ends in the afternoon around 2-3pm while the longer bus trip usually takes the whole day from 8:00 am to 6:30 pm.

**Walking Around Town – Caltrain ride from Mountain View to Atherton.**

# COMING SOON! GRAND OPENING

## Johnna M. Laird FCSN Dream Builders Reporter & Parent, Dec 2016

### *FCSN South Bay Center is coming!*

There's no place like home! No more moving equipment back-and-forth. No more having to think where to go. FCSN South Bay now has a place of its own, following an 18-month renovation that has transformed a commercial building into a permanent community center.

"We've been renting a church facility for our South Bay Center up until now. We have run our biweekly family gatherings in a separate location. As of January 2017, we will bring all our South Bay operations under one roof with rooms to grow for the foreseeable future," explains Jim Chiao, FCSN's Vice President of Operations & Volunteers, who organized project volunteers and headed some design teams.

The project was a group effort by many within FCSN, both management team and volunteers. Finding the right location took the site search committee two years. In 2014, after the Bascom property was purchased, a functional design team worked with an architect to determine the building's most functional layout. A store team determined coffee shop requirements. By late 2014, the renovation project was approved by the San Jose city planning department. Construction and interior design teams were formed to support the project until building completion. One volunteer, Mandy Chang, a designer from MGI, spent more than 800 hours on the building's interior design.

Building features include a workshop where FCSN clients can learn arts and crafts, participate in job training, and become involved in small business ventures, like soap-making. A coffee shop and store will provide an opportunity for clients to gain skills in serving the public. In addition to a multipurpose room, the center includes four classrooms, two offices, a conference room, and a computer room. As with any homeowner moving into a new location, FCSN South Bay has needs, including therapy equipment, computers and related peripherals as well as some furnishings and a television. Donations are needed.

The new facility will also become home to the Harvest Academy which provides training for higher functioning clients in skills aimed at employment.

"South Bay Center is another milestone in our journey to build a community for our children and adults with special needs and their families. Our South Bay families have been longing for and have held this dream for some time, and now we are finally able to fulfill that need," says Jim.

"And we are proud of the community support we received for the South Bay Center," says Dr. Albert Wang, who headed a construction team that included Stanley Woo and David Tu.

"With community support, we raised $1.5 million in three galas to cover renovation, furniture, and equipment costs. It shows FCSN's reputation out there as a trustworthy and efficient organization with strong leadership."

FCSN opened its first community center in 2006, having built the 6,000 square-foot Dream Center on Peralta Boulevard in Fremont.

About three-and-one half times bigger than the former rental space, the new South Bay location is expected to lead to expanded programs. Its central location on South Bascom, within blocks of San Jose City College, is expected to help FCSN gain name recognition and develop more collaborative programs with other organizations and businesses.

In late October 2016, the contractor for the South Bay project, ACON, completed construction which began in April 2015. By November 6, 2016, the City of San Jose completed inspections and issued an occupancy permit for 140 people. South Bay held its first Family Seminar Series in the new center on November 19. By mid-November a Community Care Licensing preliminary permit was issued, clearing the way for programs serving consumers to be held at the site.

Grand opening of the single-story, 8,000 square foot building located at 1029 South Bascom Ave., is slated for early 2017.

# CHAPTER 5:
# FCSN 20th Anniversary

FCSN was founded in 1996 and 2016 happens to be our 20th anniversary. Just as a toddler growing up into an adulthood, FCSN has grown from a handful of families in 1996 to over 800 hundred families in 2016. Started as a family support group, we are now an organization with branches in family support, enrichment programs, and vendorized services – a combination that is unique and not commonly found in other similar organizations. Above all, FCSN remained an organization with a clear goal and direction set by the parents of special needs families.

In 2016 edition of FCSN Newsletter, we published a special section to celebrate FCSN's 20th anniversary, and many articles are recaptured here in this chapter. One exception is Jim Chiao's article on "How FCSN Got Its Name", which can be found in chapter 1. In the first article of this chapter, Johnna Laird, FCSN parent and reporter, interviewed several co-founders who recalled the early days of the organization and the steady growth of the organization. Anna Wang, Linmei Chiao, and past chair Limin Hu, also each contributed an article to share their own personal stories. In the last article of this chapter, Johnna Laird reflected on FCSN history, her own experience, and pondered on the question of "Finding FCSN's Pioneering Spirit Today".

# FCSN FROM CRADLE TO ADULTHOOD

## Johnna M. Laird (FCSN Dream Builders Reporter & Parent), June 2016

From left – Albert Wang, Anna Wang, Linmei Chiao, Shiow-Luan Chen, Jim Chiao.

When a few pioneers gather to recount the history of Friends of Children with Special Needs, they focus on the fun they experienced.

Rather than dwell on hardships they faced to create an innovative and comprehensive program to serve people from birth through a lifetime, these pioneers laugh when they recall playgroups bringing young children together to socialize.

They remember camaraderie developed through bun sales and concert fundraisers to build the Dream Center. They remember a mall shop created to give work experience to their teens. They remember picnics, New Year's Eve celebrations, and simplifying a steamed rice recipe to teach their children step-by-step. They talk about the friendships and trust they built.

Before FCSN came into existence, Shiow-Luan Chen, a passionate teacher who was working toward a master's degree in special education from San Jose State University, worked with individual children and their parents at their homes for five years. Shiow (pronounced Show) was a lifeline when parents felt isolated.

At that time, much less was known about autism and developmental disabilities. There were few places to turn and often the places that offered help required driving long distances.

Shiow was convinced that autistic themselves and their children. Parents sat speechless as she excused herself to maintain crowd control as their children ran about, ready to play after dinner.

Many weeks passed and not much happened. Eventually, Linmei, a former special education teacher, started a conversation with Shiow about how to create movement among the families. Linmei urged participation by non-special needs families for additional help. For several months, Linmei and Shiow exchanged ideas and planned a formal meeting of the parents. They created an agenda and planned out the details. Shiow invited the Special Needs families, and Linmei invited her other friends Sheau-Yin and Peter Hsia, Amy and Jason Wang, and Joyce and Stanley Yeh. Altogether, there were about twenty families gathered at Linmei's home in April 1996. At the meeting, Shiow talked about her vision for the group, and Linmei presented a comprehensive plan. The parents were all very excited, and they all agreed to move forward. "We use the term '10 founding families' because roughly ten families were the core group that contributed to form the organization and make things happen over the years," explains Jim Chiao.

The April 1996 meeting laid out the foundation for FCSN today with integrated family support as opposed to delivering services to special needs individuals without including the family. The parent cooperative model required families to invest time and money to insure a successful future for their children.

The April 1996 meeting also included a proposal for teenagers to earn community service credits in a meaningful, educational way working with special needs children. From the beginning, founders wanted to include families whose children did not have special needs.

A planning committee was formed to carry out the formation of the parent support group. The ten founding families launched with integrated playgroups as the backbone of their children's activity. The next year, 1997, was formative. They expanded the first integrated playgroup to an all-inclusive, biweekly Family Gathering, which combined integrated classes, parent seminars, and social hours – there was something for everyone in the family. By year's end, about fifty families were attending the Family Gathering.

Moms focused on playgroups and support groups, getting parents to identify the needs of their children. The dads worked on many miscellaneous tasks. Friends, without special needs children, played the supportive role. They participated in meetings, helped in cooking, security, and accounting. "They were the glue that bonded all the families together. They were also growing their numbers," says Jim Chiao.

For the first year, the grassroots' parent cooperative held classes in each other's homes and either taught children themselves or recruited others. A social worker, Su-Ti from Asia Pacific Family Resource Center in San Jose, offered help in late 1996; as a result, FCSN began meeting at the Asia Pacific Resource Center in San Jose in February 1997 for meetings and Family Gatherings. Once local programs began in 1999, FCSN members were back using their own homes or borrowed space for meetings.

Beginning in 1998, there were more than 100 member families, prompting the creation of Mother Gathering, where moms met. It was at one of these meetings that the mothers expressed the need for programs closer to home. Based on these needs, Anna created the first "Local Program" by geographic area in Milpitas in 1999 which was quickly followed by Almaden and Saratoga groups. Local groups met by age groups at local churches, YMCAs, recreation centers, and even a dental office. Dads were meeting, too, but talking about the experience of parenting a child with special needs was challenging. "They couldn't hold back the tears and they didn't want to cry in front of other guys. It was just too sensitive, too close to home, not something they could handle in front of an audience," recalls Anna Wang.

During the first two years, meetings were held often by the planning committee, along with debates and discussions that formed the foundation of FCSN. Early on they faced a decision of whether to go alone or fold into another organization, less broadly focused. Although they did not know exactly where they were headed, these families decided to continue on the path to develop an organization reflecting their values. These were immigrants who had come to the U.S. from Asia, bringing with them a culture of self-reliance.

They developed the mission statement that still drives the organization today: "to help individuals with special needs and their families to find love, hope, respect, and support through integrated community involvement."

They searched for a name to capture the essence of the program they were evolving, but none seemed suitable until Linmei and Jim Chiao were walking out of the Saratoga Library one day. Jim's eyes fixed on a plaque with the words "Friends of Saratoga Library." Friends of Children with Special Needs won unanimous support.

In early 1999, FCSN was ready to discuss a five-year and ten-year plan at the board meetings. At the January board meeting, Linmei proposed creating a special needs community as a long-term goal.

Several board members thought the idea was too far-fetched and impractical; others thought it was an impossible dream. Half-jokingly, the board adopted the name, "Dream Community" as a long-term goal. The Dream Community was intended to place special needs individuals at the center of the community. The Dream Project evolved from the Dream Community; the first phase of the Dream Project was building the Dream Center, followed by a second phase to build programs once construction was complete.

At this point, Dr. Albert Wang became more active, stepping up and drawing on his fund-raising experience for American Cancer Society campaigns. Then one of Albert's golfing buddies, developer John Wong, offered to sell 1.5 acres on Peralta Boulevard. Disagreements about the wisdom of buying land ensued. Not everyone thought this a wise move. In two weeks' time, however, 26 families took out loans, borrowed from relatives and/or jockeyed their finances to amass $860,000 to purchase the land.

"We didn't know how, but we believed we could build a center," recalls Albert.

There was a faith among the group that what they needed would materialize. A warehouse full of dim sum buns were offered to the FCSN when an owner decided to close his business. This was an opportunity to fundraise. The bun expiration date was only two months away. Within FCSN, pessimism could be heard. "These buns won't sell," given the timing after 9-11. Moms mobilized, and the buns sold for $8 a box. Moms talked to friends and contacted local store owners. Their sales, they explained, would help realize their dreams for their children. Before the eight weeks ended, every bun had been sold and $12,000 was generated by FCSN's first fundraiser.

The next year, 2002, FCSN held its first gala with assistance from Citizens for a Better Community, a Fremont-based organization. Limin Hu, relatively new at FCSN, volunteered to chair the event. His organizational skills were put to the test, but he did not disappoint. The first gala turned out to be a huge success. Bun-buyers were in the audience, having established a bond with Friends of Children with Special Needs. The gala was established as an annual fundraiser. There were also three fundraising concerts, bringing cultural Taiwanese folk music to the Bay Area.

"I think we learned that when the time is right, things will happen," recalls Anna, whose family was among the ten. "Often, we tried to make things happen, and they just would not. When the stars align, things happen. That's how it was with the Dream Project. We had to take a leap of faith."

It took almost six years for the Dream Center to be built. There were meetings to rezone property and subdivide it. When families met with their prospective Peralta Boulevard neighbors, parents brought their children who served cookies and shook their future neighbors' hands.

"They didn't have the heart to say no to us," recalls Linmei.

"I just think of it as higher planning from above," says Albert Wang. "The Big Guy picked the time, and we ran with it."

"God sent us all these angels," says Anna.

John Wong was one of them, when he sold the land to Peralta Dream Limited Liability Corporation, parent investors. The land sale, Wong admits, was because of his relationship and respect for Anna and Albert.

"I had no idea Anna and Albert could do so much for our community and FCSN children," says Wong. "I am honored to be a small part of FCSN efforts. FCSN organizers are role models in our community..."

Leadership, and a strong board made up of families, has contributed to FCSN's success. During the first two years, FCSN was guided by a planning committee led by Shiow, Peter Hsia and Linmei. In 1998, FCSN set up its first Board of Directors which in turn elected Linmei as its first chairperson/president. The next year in 1999, Tsai-Wei Wu served for a year. From 1999 to 2006, Albert Wang served three terms as president, followed by Anna and Limin Hu who assumed the presidential responsibilities. Jim Chiao became president in 2006 for one term before Tsai-Wei took the reins of president. With its building completed, FCSN launched phase two to build programs. With Sylvia Yeh, Linmei Chiao, Anna Wang, Josephine Chou as key management staff and Lillian Lin as volunteer, FCSN launched Supported Living Services, Adult Day Program, and a host of local programs in the East Bay. In 2007, Tsai-Wei began an unprecedented six terms as president. During his tenure he formalized FCSN's organizational structure and set a growth path for FCSN programs. By 2013, FCSN had reached maximum capacity at 200 adult students in FCSN's vendored programs, served by 100 staff members.

Lives of special needs individuals changed because of FCSN, but the lives of their parents changed as well.

"This experience led me into a different world. I could have been talking with people about stocks and investing," says Linmei, "and name-brand purses. Instead, we are telling touching stories, helping each other. My son, Brian, took me into a totally different world and I am better for it."

# 20TH ANNIVERSARY AND TRANSFORMATION OF FCSN

Limin Hu (Former Chair of Board of Directors), June 2016

When you come to a fork in the road, take it.

– by Yogi Berra

Congratulations to Friends of Children with Special Needs for the 20th Anniversary and for the tremendous growth and transformation into "adulthood." I have been fortunate to participate and witness the beautiful journey of FCSN and also, the journey of my own son, Dennis, now twenty years old. I'd like to share the stories of FCSN and Dennis growing through Childhood, Youth, and Adolescence.

In 1996, FCSN was formed by a group of ten families, with the mission to build a village to help each other to raise children with special needs, including Down syndrome, autism, and other types of developmental delay. In the first six years, FCSN had become a great group of parents, volunteers and educators, with seminars, local programs, and parents' support groups. I would describe this as the "Childhood" phase.

During this "Childhood" phase, I felt my life was shattered by the discovery that my second son, Dennis, is autistic. After countless hours of research on the Internet and with books, I felt my heart sink deeper and deeper because there is NO cure. At that time, I had launched three start-up companies in parallel, wanting to be the next Bill Gates. (Well, today I probably should change my idol to Mark Zuckerberg.) As an immigrant struggling to survive and build my own career, I was really overwhelmed by the conflicting goals of building my career to make money to support my son and dedicating my life to help my son to grow. Then I remembered Yogi Berra's saying, "Just take it." I had decided that early intervention was the key, and I would simply do my best to help Dennis to develop to his full potential.

At that point, I found FCSN to be the beacon in my darkest days. FCSN provided much needed information, guidance, and support, but even more importantly I got to know the wonderful people at FCSN. Somehow, knowing that I was not alone brightened my own struggle. After two years of intensive at-home behavior program, a miracle happened, and Dennis started to talk. At the age of four-and-half, he finally opened his mouth and called me "Dad." That was one of the happiest moments in my life.

In 2001, FCSN entered the second phase – "Youth". Albert Wang and I both felt that it was almost impossible for parents like us to face this kind of challenge by ourselves, despite the fact that both of us are reasonably resourceful. We had the conviction that FCSN's vision to build a village with community support needed to be spread, and we wanted to "Dream the Impossible Dreams." FCSN launched the Dream Project to build a one-of-a-kind FCSN Center in Fremont. In the five years that followed, we raised $3 million, mostly from small donations in the Chinese community; FCSN rallied support from all areas and dedicated itself to build a center in Fremont, opening the new building and launching programs in 2006.

In the next few years, Tsai-Wei Wu served as President, and I served as Chairman of the Board. Mostly to Tsai-Wei's credit, we were building a strong foundation for FCSN to become a well-orga-nized, self-sustaining (i.e. profitable) charity organization to serve the increasingly larger population of children and adults with special needs. We were getting recognition as one of the best run non-profit organizations, not only in the Chinese community but also in main-stream society as well. We have served and helped hundreds of children and adults and their families to find love, hope, and respect. Kudos to hundreds of staff and volunteers!

In recent years, FCSN has entered "Adolescence" phase, on its way to becoming a grown-up. The key challenge is to maintain the focus on culture and people. At the end, we want to deliver happiness by daring to dream and pursuing excellence through innovation, and yet remaining open, positive, and fun, respecting each other. This is the only way to grow and expand FCSN.

Under the leadership of volunteer President Jim Chiao and Yee-Yeen Wang, FCSN created core values and helped blend the center operation with paid staff members and volunteer programs. Sylvia Yeh, Lilian Lin, and Anna Wang all worked diligently with staff and volunteers to further the progression of FCSN. Working as a team and as a family, FCSN can look forward to the next milestone – the upcoming Grand Opening of our South Bay FCSN Center in San Jose.

Looking back to the past twenty years, FCSN united many families and helped many children to experience a full life. Not every special kid can grow up to be an engineer or an office worker, but they can learn to take care of themselves and be productive citizens of the society.

Just look at what the Dream Achiever Band and Special Need Talent Shows have accomplished.

FCSN will continue to grow and flourish in the future. And my son, Dennis, is now living independently and studying accounting in San Jose State University. After all, life is good.

# FCSN AND I: LIVES CHANGED

### Linmei Chiao (Former FCSN President, Co-founder, and Parent), June 2016

The Chiao Family.

Can't believe FCSN is reaching its 20th anniversary and has become such a fine, fully-grown non-profit organization.

Back in 1996, the year FCSN was born, I was a busy high tech working mom with two kids and a busy engineer husband. My daughter was in Saratoga High, and my special-needs son in Argonaut Elementary School.

Life was hectic with a full-time job, kids' activities, some investment, and endless housework. However, when my son's Sunday school teacher/ godmother, Ms. Shiow-Luan Chen, who was also a special education teacher, suggested that parents with special needs children should form a support group, somehow the idea injected great energy in me.

I still remember how I stayed up late to prepare for FCSN's inception meeting on 4/6/1996 at my Saratoga home. Even now, closing my eyes, I can still feel the excitement when at the end of the meeting, the twenty attending families decided to go ahead with forming a non-profit organization. A Planning Committee was established with Shiow and Peter Hsia (a friend experienced in running non-profits) serving as advisors. I'm forever thankful that FCSN has since enriched and became a big part of my whole family's life.

During 1996-1997, in addition to joining in establishing directions for this new organization (finding a name, setting missions, bylaws, short/long term goals, etc.), I volunteered to coordinate activities and programs.

Our first event was a picnic that took place on 7/13/1996 at Linda Vista Park in Cupertino. Thanks to Chinese newspapers' reporting, many new families learned about the event and participated. I can't help but smile every time recalling the non-stop laughter during our opening group exercise "Left Twist Right Twist," all the funny ways of crawling through Sufen's creative obstacle courses, and the exciting tug-of-war.

Almost immediately following the picnic, we started to plan for the "Family Gatherings" with the idea that we need to meet regularly to build bonding between families and to provide mutual support. In preparation, we conducted "Experimental Classes" at my basement and at Sufen's house to make sure that the volunteer teachers could handle our children. We also had a Chinese New Year's party at Asian Pacific Family Resource Center (APFRC), the place where Su-Ti worked, to test out the location.

Finally, on 4/5/1997, FCSN started its first "Family Gathering," a program to bring all FCSN families together on Saturday evenings to interact closely like a big family.

I will never forget the roast whole pig Sheau-Yin brought into one of our celebrations during the Family Gathering. The whole pig got me screaming. I used a handkerchief to cover up the head. Everyone else laughed and enjoyed the delicious treat.

I also remember the lovely Mother's Day celebration at one of the gatherings. We had all the mothers escorted into beautifully decorated tables while fathers sang and performed – all those are priceless memories.

In June 1998, at the first annual meeting, the election results of the FCSN Board of Directors were announced. Shortly after, I was elected the first FCSN Chairperson/ President. During that time, with high demands, our membership grew rapidly; FCSN started to participate in many community activities such as parades, community fairs and other non-profit events. Thanks to Anna, the FCSN Mother Gathering started. With inputs from the moms, Anna also started our first Local Program in Milpitas in 1999 to support local parents' needs.

From 2001 to 2006 was the "Dream Project" era that resulted in building a brand new FCSN Center at Fremont. Under Dr. Albert Wang's leadership, Peter Hsia, Stanley Woo, Larry Peng and I formed the construction team. I took on the coordinator/secretary role and was blessed to learn so much while dealing with architects, contractors, city officials, and neighbors. Despite my nerve-wracking speeches at FCSN-hosted private neighborhood meetings and at city councils, FCSN earned the support we needed to build the Dream Center. My experiences inspired me to join the Toastmasters Club later to improve my public speaking ability.

Forming Peralta Dream LLC was another incredible experience for me. PDLLC funded PDLLC Apartments, FCSN parent sponsored housing and part of the Dream Project, to provide housing for our adult children. In addition, PDLLC also subsequently donated land for building the FCSN Center on Peralta. These families' interest and support were timely and incredible.

On the lighter side, during the first couple of FCSN Fundraising Galas, I volunteered to choreograph dances like Yellow Submarines, Kung-Fu Dance, etc.

Eventually, with the loving support from our families, staff, volunteers, donors, news media, Regional Centers, and other community partners – as if by miracle and hard work – the FCSN Center was completed and became fully operational by summer of 2006.

While the FCSN Center was under construction, starting 2004, we also worked on becoming a Regional Center's certified vendor to operate public-funded programs. During the vendor application process, I was glad to find out that my master's degree in Special Education, my teaching certificate, and my experience back in Ohio became a helpful credential in obtaining vendor certification. In September 2004, as a pilot program with Ms. Moon Chia's guidance, I started FCSN's first "South Bay Adult Day Program," funded by San Andreas Regional Center, a community-based program that mainly operated from the "FCSN Booth" (an FCSN owned small gift shop located in West San Jose/Saratoga area). While the South Bay ADP was running with support from Anna Wang, Sylvia Yeh and Lillian Lin, I also started working with professional consultants to repeat the application process with the Regional Center of the East Bay (RCEB). Finally, in 2006, FCSN also successfully became RCEB's certified vendor in Supported Living Program, Adult Day Program, and

Independent Living Program, just in time for FCSN Dream Center's opening on Peralta.

In 2006, when the Dream Center construction was completed, my husband Jim and I sold our Saratoga home and moved to the PDLLC apartment in the back of the FCSN Center. To help get things started, I took on FCSN's Supported Living Service Director position. It was truly an amazing experience to be able to live in a community with our special needs adults, to do Tai-Chi with them in the morning and join in the reading club at night, among many other activities. In 2007, after I had fulfilled my one-year commitment, I was ready to retire from the director position, and we moved out of the apartment, feeling confident that FCSN's Supported Living Services had begun and would continue.

Nowadays, Jim and I remain on the FCSN Board; Jim serves as FCSN's vice president. I enjoy being a supporter and cheerleader and still volunteering to take on specific projects that suit me. Mainly, I make myself available as an advisor/mentor to any FCSN member who can use my help. I strongly believe in the FCSN big family and will not give up in making it a loving home for our special needs families, our caring staff, and our wonderful volunteers/supporters.

My son, among many other special needs individuals, is now happily under FCSN's care through FCSN Adult Day Program and Supported Living Service programs. I, as well as many other parents, cannot thank FCSN enough for giving our children a safe and loving home and for giving parents a well-deserved, quality, retired life without worrying about our special needs sons and daughters. We thank each and every FCSN leader, staff, and volunteer. Your caring hearts and hard work are deeply valued and highly appreciated. We are also thankful for having FCSN to give us opportunities to learn, to serve, to be involved, and to love.

# HOW FCSN HAS CHANGED MY LIFE

## Anna Wang (FCSN Co-founder & VP of Local Programs), June 2016

Albert and I are proud parents of three wonderful children, two daughters and a son. Twenty-three years ago, we were devastated when our son Lawrence was diagnosed with autism. He has severe deficits in communication, socialization, and behaviors. We didn't know what to do. I thought if I had love and patience for my child, everything would work out. But I was wrong. Things were more challenging than I thought. When Lawrence had self-injurious behavior and bled, my heart bled, too. It was too painful. I felt helpless, hopeless, burnt out, and alone in my struggle. I cried silently every night wondering what our future would be.

Then twenty years ago, we met other families who shared the same passion for special needs children, although some of them did not have special needs children of their own. We understood each other's struggles and pain. We found new hope and strength in each other. Together, we started FCSN.

Our mission is to help special needs children and their families to find love, hope, and respect through integrated community involvement. FCSN started this small model of an ideal integrated community with 10 families, but we have now grown to more than 1000 member families. At FCSN, permanent friendships have developed among the children. Permanent friendships have developed among the parents, too. Many families found their home at FCSN just like mine. Our integrated activities support the well-being of entire families– mothers and fathers, brothers and sisters, grandparents, aunts and uncles, and cousins. We knew for our children to do well, the whole family has to do well. Our families worried that because of poor health, old age or death that they would be unable to support their special needs loved ones. As a result, FCSN families worked together and built a village of support to provide life-long care for our children which in turn gives families peace of mind.

We love each other's children as our own. It tugs at my heart-strings every time I hear the children and adults call me Auntie Anna. What a privilege it is to be part of so many special angels' lives! We successfully achieved the Dream Projects that provide integrated programs to children and adults, including enrichment programs, recreation, employment, and housing. We went from a grassroots volunteer organization to a well-established, full-service charity. This is a true testimony of the love and dedication of our families and staff.

Lawrence is now twenty-six. He holds three part-time jobs and performs music on the weekend with the Dream Achievers Band, a band composed of musicians with autism. He sings and plays five different instruments. So many miracles have happened in his life through FCSN that I would need to write a book to fully share his stories.

How my life has changed because of raising Lawrence and journeying with FCSN! Sometimes our lives may not turn out the way we planned only for the better. My vision was broadened, my love for all children deepened. I met so many kind and loving people, especially pure-hearted angels.

So, what seemed to be a misfortune when my son was diagnosed turned out to be my greatest blessing. Our children are truly our greatest gift.

What I want to say to all parents of special needs children is this: Never Give Up on them because they blossom at different times.

We have to create many opportunities for them.

We can build a brighter future for our children and for the special needs community.

Dreams are not broken; we just have to adopt new dreams.

Together, we can make all our dreams come true.

# FINDING FCSN'S PIONEERING
# SPIRIT TODAY

Johnna Laid (FCSN Dream Builders Reporter & Parent),
June 2016

"Give a man a fish and you feed him for a day; teach a
man to fish and you feed him for a lifetime." Maimonides

Articles throughout this newsletter celebrate FCSN's twenty-year
anniversary. A relative newcomer to the FCSN community, I marvel
at the grassroots beginning of Friends of Children with Special Needs.
A handful of parents met in a living room with a commitment to
give their children the best lives possible. At some level they knew
to do that, they needed support. They didn't look outside themselves
but from within the group, empowering each other and each other's children.

These first FCSN families didn't have a roadmap, but they had a
vision. They envisioned an "ideal integrated community" built upon
the foundation of "love, hope and respect" that guided them. They
believed so powerfully in that possibility that they never veered, com-
promised, or gave up.

What strength powered them? Determination? Fortitude?
Commitment? They didn't always agree on the process, but their
mission unified them. While creating the community of FCSN, they
managed careers, families with multiple children, and professional
responsibilities, all while advancing their dream a step at a time.
In some ways, their success which blesses my life and many others,
reminds me of a line from the movie, Field of Dreams: "If you build
it, they will come."

FCSN has become a magnet for families who want a quality experience for their loved ones with special needs, offering interesting, engaging, and growthful opportunities that help children and adults feel vital, productive, and joyful about life.

Growth has led to a vibrant, expansive FCSN program that far exceeds its pioneering days of playgroups and parents hosting classes in their homes, but the beginning days held the essential seeds of FCSN's mission today.

The challenge in the coming decades is to remember that FCSN began as a parent cooperative, designed to empower families and special needs individuals. In the years ahead, how does the FCSN community maintain that entrepreneurial, growth-minded spirit within a well-respected, multi-million dollar nonprofit that meets and exceeds state and federal standards in service to special needs individuals? When an organization reaches FCSN's size, there is a temptation to think "oh, FCSN, the organization, will do it."

When my daughter, Kendra, was accepted into FCSN in 2013, I thought of FCSN as an "organization," like a business, where I dropped her off and picked her up and interfaced with staff when called upon to do so. My experience with previous programs trained me that parents were often kept on the periphery. I didn't have a handbook that told me how to function as a parent within vendored programs; I was so over-the-moon excited to have Kendra at FCSN I didn't want to do anything to make waves. I saw parents involved, but I didn't understand how this happened. I did not understand until recently that FCSN operates with the heart of a parent cooperative, despite being a Regional Center vendor with all that it entails. I am learning that FCSN needs parents to find ways to contribute, building upon the success of the last two decades.

Sometimes when grassroots organizations reach this level of success, new parents coming in, unaware of the grassroots history, believe the work is accomplished by "the organization."

I am learning that FCSN's community is a triad: a caring skillful staff; capable and creative consumers; and involved parents, vested in guiding the future for their and all special needs' children. Together, the three create a powerful triangle.

My daughter's life improved so much after moving to FCSN, but there are changes that could lead to a more fulfilled life. I feel, however, that I don't know how to create those changes.

I wonder if the answer lies within group-mind, smaller groups within the community, parents who experience similar needs meeting to create solutions. Already a group has begun to meet to discuss creating a second wave of community housing for their children, the way parents invested to build the Peralta Dream Limited Liability Corporation.

Rather than look to the "organization," I wonder if looking to the group would empower me and fuel me with the FCSN pioneering spirit.

# CHAPTER 6:
# Fulfill Our Dream
## (2017-2019)

After two years of renovation work, in April of 2017, FCSN opened its South Bay Center at Bascom Ave in San Jose. The Center filled up quickly with our South Bay Adult Day Program and a host of children and family programs. The Center provided a home for our special needs programs and fulfilled a commitment to our South Bay member families.

In addition, in 2018, FCSN opened Friends Coffee and Tea at the same location. The coffee shop provides job training opportunities for our clients; it is also a place to display our clients' crafts and artworks – what they can do. In many ways, it opens a window between us and our neighborhood and the community at large.

2017-2019 was also a period of transition in the leadership. After a two years stint as president, in 2017, Yee-Yeen Wang shared the position with Jim Chiao as co-presidents. When Yee-Yeen retired in 2018, Jim shared the co-president position with CK Lee. By 2019, CK became the sole president.

# TWO YEARS IN THE MAKING, DECADES IN FAMILIES' HEARTS

## Kenneth Song (FCSN Dream Builders Reporter), June 2017

**Ribbon cutting ceremony during FCSN South Bay Center's grand opening. (2017)**

Widely recognized for its successful community-based approach to support families with special needs individuals, FCSN achieved a significant milestone with the grand opening of its South Bay Dream Center. First envisioned over ten years ago, the San Jose center has been a demanding group project, long in the works. On April 26th, hundreds of esteemed guests including government officials, school board members, community partners, and sponsors from all over the Bay Area joined FCSN families, volunteers, and staff to commemorate this extraordinary occasion. Celebrating the organization's success in providing a stable growing environment for special needs individuals of all ages, the grand opening offered the greater community a clear message of hope for the future.

After weeks of planning and hard work, parents, volunteers, and staff arrived bright and early in the morning to help prepare a wide assortment of sandwiches, cookies, and other refreshments in the kitchen. Various displays of student-made art and products ranging from soaps and chocolates to paper-woven baskets and glazed pottery were set up throughout the building. In addition, Chi-Ling Wu, a client and talented musician, performed beautifully on the piano in the background – making the experience of just strolling through the facilities a wonderfully varied showcase of the incredible talents being cultivated at FCSN.

When the guests arrived, they were invited to explore the facility on one of many guided tours, all led by excited clients and parents eager to show off their new home. From the multi-purpose auditorium where the guests initially entered to the various classrooms decorated with works from students, the computer room, conference rooms where family support seminars were held, and a big training room with utility for ceramic and soap making classes, it was evident just how much effort and care had gone into the design and construction of this 8,000 square foot building.

As everyone gathered outside for the ribbon cutting ceremony, the percussion band started off with a lively performance which put everyone in a festive mood. Nearly 30 VIP guests lined up behind the thick, red ribbon decorated with many flowery bows. Upon Chairman Dr. Chenming Hu's command, the grand opening red ribbon was cut amidst bombastic applause, and guests were ushered inside for the opening ceremony.

To start off the ceremony, Chairman Hu acknowledged all the various individuals, families, and organizations that have made FCSN's success possible. A brief presentation with photos of the center during various stages of renovation took the audience through the center's transformation over the last two years. Awards were presented to key individuals from the project design and construction teams, accompanied by numerous rounds of applause from the audience.

The many individuals who spoke all shared a common feeling of deep pride for being able to support a community which has accomplished so much in the past twenty-one years. During his speech, President Yee-Yeen Wang emphasized how much FCSN has grown as a service platform for aiding parents in identifying the gaps in their children's learning abilities, and how FCSN has developed a solid foundation for setting up programs to address those issues. As the organization has always relied on the ideas and ingenuity of the parents who truly know their children best, FCSN will continue to strive to discover new and innovative paths in special needs education.

Chairman Hu concluded the ceremony by saying, "Our vision is to build a community for children and adults with special needs, and you are an important part of the community, and we look forward to continue the dream with you." This grand opening celebration was a huge success and great accomplishment of all members and friends of FCSN!

**Chenming, board members, and volunteers stood ready to conduct tours during South Bay Center grand opening. (2017)**

# FCSN SOUTH BAY PERCUSSION GROUP

Sufen Wu (FCSN parent, translated by Paul Song from Chinese), June 2017

The Beginning: When my son Chi-Ling turned 23 in 2013, he naturally entered FCSN's Day Program. That was the year I met Teacher Amy.

Amy is a piano teacher full of love. She is never satisfied with her teaching of many gifted and excellent students, and she always hopes that her students can accomplish more. In addition to enriching their own lives with music, she teaches them to also prevail in other areas. Therefore, helping disadvantaged groups became an important goal in her life plan. Sparks ignited between us immediately when we met! Music was our greatest intersection.

Almost every day in the summer of 2014, Amy led her group of students in one-on-one piano lessons for FCSN students interested in music during the Day Program. Also, she was particularly willing to teach some children with lower function in music; she even set up a special group and taught them to use shaker, drumstick, or other simple instruments for creating beats. For many students who required additional attention and assistance, she wrote lyrics on poster board to enhance the visual input. She spent at least four hours a week in the classroom so students could continuously practice. Amy always bought a lot of snacks to reward children. Throughout the summer, her middle and high school students also continuously accompanied our special need students to prepare for the Benefit Concert in October. It was incredible how much they wanted to bring these FCSN students to the show stage!

After a burst of intense training and preparation, the first FCSN fundraising Benefit Concert was held in mid-October. This program raised more than three thousand dollars for FCSN! In the same year, the Christmas Concert raised another four thousand dollars. Who says special needs have no power?

During the second year, we found that one-on-one piano lessons were not as effective and unintentionally put a lot of pressure on the children. So we changed plans and moved toward an integrated way to reduce the pressure of learning. That is, we mainly focused on group learning. Since learning a melody the old-fashioned way was not feasible or practical for these children, then how about percussion instruments? This was a challenge for Teacher Amy with her piano background! So, she started drum lessons on her own; and one month later, Dr. Hsieh was introduced into our classroom! Teacher Hsieh had a lot of good ideas! In the first lesson he made the students know that music is everywhere: all things around us such as pots, bowls, spoons, even trash cans be used as music material. So, we temporarily got out of the music notes and jumped into the percussion world.

In order to practice playing with trash cans, parents donated excess trash cans from home; 30 gallons or 15 gallons, red or black, treble or bass, borrowed or bought, we gathered them all together so every student would have something to play. The big trash can was used for playing bass; the small, medium, mini-sized barrels, laundry pods, and even brooms all had their own contributions to our percussion program. This reminded us of the old days, doing busy works in the countryside, people washing, brushing, cutting, mixing, knocking, tapping, and making all kinds of random sound. By listening carefully, on-lookers could actually find order within the chaos, just like a needle in embroidery work. With the first glance there is no regular expression; only by focusing the senses can one glimpse and grasp the true presentation of art.

One performance took the teachers, assistants, and parents a lot of preparation efforts – every week children practiced at least once and each time at least one hour. The parents eagerly participated as they became teaching assistants, so every student had individual supervision and guidance. Big trash cans for bass play at slower beat; it may sound easy, but this actually requires great physical strength. Small and medium-sized barrels are used to play half notes or even faster quarter or eight notes. Often, we needed group practices for coordination. So for a while we walked in school like a group dedicated to garbage collection. The biggest advantage of such a big sound is that no one can relax or fake playing. A wrong beat can be so noticeable that anyone who makes such a mistake will feel embarrassed and difficult to forgive himself; this pushes everyone to practice harder.

Furthermore, we discovered that the body can also be an instrument! Under the guidance of Teacher Hsieh, everyone used their hands to make sound by hitting their own body, from shoulder down to calf, then from ankle up to chest as if they were doing self-massage. The more sophisticated massage performers such as Teacher Amy, usually found herself with purple marks all over her thighs, and she could only comfort herself through exercise to help blood circulation. We all discovered that this kind of music class actually includes physical education at the same time. In addition to the practiced coordination of eyes and ears, everyone used every inch of muscle, so it can be thought of as killing two birds with one stone.

After "full body" exercise, we gradually advanced further. Teacher Hsieh utilized more instruments to enrich our percussion music. So, shaker, tambourine, even timbalie, floortom, and AGoGo bell were used. Everyone worked together to find more professional props. After a few months of practice, we accomplished a new song, *Samba Way*. This song, from Brazilian carnival music, makes people want to dance involuntarily; the beat of this music touches and resonates within every heart. It immediately grasps the audience's warm passions so they dance involuntarily, experiencing the exciting rhythm of Latin music. The South Bay Percussion made such a wonderful and impressive performance at the Family Day that our FCSN family was deeply impressed.

After the Family Day in June, we continued moving forward. When our team's beat rhythm became more mature, this became the right time to add some music! So, our band became more like a real percussion band. Then the teachers, students and parents once again assembled and worked together. We moved all the possible instruments (that we could find, borrow, or purchase) into the classroom: items such as bells, a xylophone, and a marimba. After only about a month, the classroom atmosphere changed from Brazil music style to Taiwan folksong, *"Diu Diu Tong Ah"* minor tunestyle diffused classroom, and our mighty Teacher Hsieh merged two totally different styles of music together, combining both the passionate and implicit simple styles of each. Music, as described by either Xu ZhiMo or Zhu ZiQing who said, "It has feet!" It gave us a feeling of riding a train from the fine, grass and breezy shore of the Eastern world to the hot, dazzling Latin America. This song called *"Take a Samba Train"* dazzled during our FCSN 20-year Gala celebration.

South Bay percussion is a music group composed of many students from the South Bay ADP class. Since student music levels or attainment differ, the only thing they share is their interest in music – when their eyes light up hearing musical rhythm.

The consensus of Teacher Amy and our parents is that all children who are interested in and willing to accept the teachers' guidance can participate in this music program. Everyone has the right to enjoy and learn music. This is an all-inclusive group; every student can achieve his or her individual goal according to his or her different ability and devotion. The right to enjoy music in the kingdom of music is equal. If we took the elite system, and only picked the better performing students, then we would never have discovered that Alan – who could not keep up with the instructions – created strange but wonderful and marvelous sounds. He put such a great heat and passion in his performance; he burst out with most enthusiastic cheers at the end of a beat. His solo play presents his most excellent self. In addition, Tony was a very shy child who rarely responded to other people, but when he played solo with Alan, he suddenly transformed into a totally different person with great pride and self-confidence. Recently, we noticed another child, Christopher, who never interacted with other people. Yet, after he began to play the shakers, even though he still did not talk, he learned to express his voice. When music lessons were over, Christopher actively helped me pick up drumsticks and cover the xylophone. This achievement – turning from nothing to something – makes us very excited. This progress also made many parents want to enter this music program. This is our goal to make the music program the highlight of our South Bay Day Program.

This year, Teacher Hsieh has added more music elements and complex rhythms to our program. In our music class, teachers, children, and parents are making every effort twice a week to practice the beat with their children. We continue to correct all mistakes, over and over, until our goal is accomplished. Parents such as Xiaoman, Lillian, and Jennifer take homework home every week to keep up with practice, hoping that the next time their children could perform better. With such a spirit to overcoming all obstacles, I believe our performance this year will be even more incredible.

Finally, I would like to pay the highest respect to Teacher Amy. Without her company along the road, we never would have succeeded. Like Santa Claus, she always brings refreshments and prizes to encourage students and other teachers. During the past few years, she has become the most popular volunteer in class. Once again, our deepest thanks to Teacher Amy. Without an initiator like her, we could never have formed such a large band. Most importantly of all, we are able to provide opportunities for all children who enjoy music.

Let's go, SBADP!

# HARVEST ACADEMY PROGRAM OPENS IN SOUTH BAY

Kenneth Song (FCSN Dream Builders Reporter), Dec 2017

*Empowering Students Toward Employment*

Over the past 20 years, Friends of Children with Special Needs has worked relentlessly to carve a place in the community for those with special needs to create a place of belonging as well as provide a sense of identity. While many special needs individuals have the functional skill set to work in advanced, even technical workplaces, it is often the twin barriers of communication and an educational degree which discourage them from reaching their full potential. Such is the case within our own local Bay Area, flourishing with job opportunities for those with the right talents, yet even exceptional special needs individuals such as those with high-functioning autism (HFA) and

Asperger's Syndrome (AS) are finding it difficult to compete in a system with which they are unfamiliar. Started this past June by Mrs. Hsin Huei Liao, Ms. Sherry Meng, and Ms. Teresa Yu, the Harvest Academy Program aims to develop the skills that individuals with high functioning autism or Asperger's syndrome require to perform in a college or workplace environment. They hope to empower individuals with high functioning autism to have confidence in themselves to succeed, even when society presents barriers.

Offering a diverse curriculum ranging from computer applications and accounting to social etiquette and drama courses, the Harvest Academy Program aims to build a strong academic foundation with critical communication and social training integrated into every class. Ultimately, the skills which students develop over the course of the quarter will build toward three distinct goals: academic tutoring toward a college level of education; job training for a career in the tech industry; and community skill development to represent the special needs population positively. The program's highly qualified team of enthusiastic instructors who come from top universities around the country including UC Davis, Berkeley, and Columbia University work closely with the students in small class sizes with flexible curriculums to meet each student's unique needs. Several teachers also have extensive backgrounds working with special needs individuals and have the essential qualities of patience and empathy needed to bring out the best in their students.

I had the privilege of sitting through several, different classes including Functional English, Communications, and Drama during the Fall 2016 quarter. While each class focused on a different aspect of a student's growth, such as learning how to use computers, how to interact in public, and how to write out their thoughts, all classes built upon a common theme of expanding students' confidence and ability to perform in social settings. Speaking with the various instructors, I learned that the teaching staff actually creates each weekly lesson plan from scratch, an arduous but rewarding process that involves integrating feedback from the students and their parents. By constantly adjusting and tweaking the curriculum on a class-by-class basis, instructors are able to emphasize the challenge areas and help each individual student work through their struggle. This fluidity in the speed and topics covered by each course is what truly gives the Harvest Academy Program an edge over traditional classes that mechanically aim to complete a preset amount of materials before the last day of class.

Prospective students who wish to apply for the Harvest Academy Program need to undergo an interview process to assess their strengths and weaknesses before determining whether they are a good fit for the current level of the class. The program committee, consisting of the program founders and 5 teachers, then separates the students based on their level and preferred schedule into the appropriate classes. Each course has a maximum class size of four to six students to allow each instructor to tailor the curriculum to each student's own pace. Between the instructors and helpful volunteers who assist throughout each class, students are given the one-on-one attention they need to stay focused and excel throughout the hour. Teresa Yu, Program Manager of Harvest Academy Program, also spends much of her time reaching out to both local and global organizations, including Specialisterne and Expandability, to arrange potential job partnerships with graduates from the Harvest Academy Program. In recent years, such companies have shown a widening interest in looking toward the unique temperament and skillset of the special needs community for employees in accounting, programming, and much more. As the program continues to produce well-prepared graduates who are trained to handle a work environment, Teresa anticipates that more companies will become interested in partnering up with the Harvest Academy Program.

With only two quarters under the organization's belt so far, the progress many of its students have made in such a short period of time looks extremely promising for the future of special needs education. Throughout the course of these first two quarters, Mrs. Liao reports that she has seen an impressive shift in the mentality of her students who have become much more serious and responsible regarding their own education.

I recently had the pleasure of attending the fall graduation ceremony and open house where students showcased their achievements over the past quarter. Between the spectacular performance of The Tortoise and the Hare, which drama instructor Valerie Peterson brought to life with five students who once would have never dared to perform in front of an audience, and massive binders of Excel, math, English, and communications exercises the students had completed throughout the quarter, it was an impressive display of learning and progress to say the least.

With each quarter that passes, the Harvest Academy Program not only builds upon its past experiences to optimize student education but also continues to broaden its class catalog to offer courses for special needs individuals of all backgrounds and interests. Expanded functional English and math courses for a wider range of skill levels, one-on-one tutoring sessions, cheerleading classes, and a core drama team are among the exciting elements already integrated into the program. Mrs. Liao encourages parents who may not believe that their special needs child are capable of attaining a college degree or full time employment to have faith in their children and to never give up. Only by driving such individuals on a daily basis and giving them the independence to pursue their own careers can individuals truly recognize their capabilities and full potential.

# FCSN FAMILY FUN FESTIVAL

Kelly Ko (East Bay Enrichment Program Manager), Dec 2017

*An Outreach Event sponsored by the Regional Center*

This year, in an effort to outreach to the Asian community, the Regional Center partnered with and sponsored FCSN to host the very first Family Fun Festival at the Always Dream Play Park located at Fremont's Central Park (Lake Elizabeth). The event took place on Sunday, August 27, 2017, from 11:00am to 3:00pm. FCSN was chosen because many of FCSN's members and families are Asian. Regional Center has a commitment to cultural and linguistic sensitivity to the needs and struggles of the Asian community, which is a target audience for the Regional Center. At FCSN, we were super excited to be chosen. Events like these give FCSN an opportunity to educate Asian families about Regional Center and the services it provides.

As one of the outreach managers, I had the pleasure of planning this special event with the help of my wonderful staff. The month-long planning included creating and distributing flyers in English, Chinese and Vietnamese; we invited community partners to provide resource information; we purchased food, packaged giveaway bags, and thought of different game ideas. We also recruited volunteers. There were so many details we needed to plan. It was satisfying to see all aspects come together on the day of the event.

It was a fun-filled day with free food, carnival games, face-painting, a jump house, bubble station, arts and craft, raffle drawings, and even a manicure station. Although temperatures soared into the mid-90s, more than 400 people attended. Over 80% of attendees were Asians We counted more than 150 families who supported our event. Each family who came and signed in received free FCSN drawstring bags filled with school supplies. Some community partners, including Disability Rights California Bay Area, Asian Pacific Islander American Public Affairs, Regional Center of the East Bay, San Andreas Regional Center, Developmental Disability Council, and Voter Registration among others, hosted a booth at the source fair to share information about their organizations.

A huge thank you to Auntie Anna Wang, Vice President of Enrichment Programs and Community Relations, for coordinating live entertainment enjoyed throughout the day. She invited finalists and winners from our 2017 Special Needs Talent Showcase to perform, and the performers put on an amazing show. Performances reflected the diverse cultures within our community. Attendees were able to see and enjoy the talents on stage. The Music Camp Band opened the show with *"Fanfare," "Spy Medley,"* and *"That's What Friends Are For."* Other performances included Laurie Chu's scarf dance, Julian Huang's instrumental music performed on the piano, Rod Rodriguez and Lynn Pisco's hip-hop dances, Dream Seekers' singing and dancing, among others.

Great cultural performance was given by Jasmine Dan, who performed an Indian dance, while Ria Sachdev, sang an Indian song. Chiling Wu played the piano and Chinese dulcimer. The performance concluded with The Music Camp Band's "*We are the World.*"

Ten FCSN staff members and more than 30 volunteers from FCSN and Global Leadership Initiative contributed time to help us set up and clean up, run all the games and booths, and serve the food to guests. I want to especially thank a few of these people for their extra hard work.

Thank you to Uncle James Gong for cooking a scrumptious lunch consisting of different types of burgers and hot dogs under the scorching sun, Auntie Anna and Ping Ding for transporting everything from the Fremont Center to the play park, and the After-school Program staff for overseeing and working the FCSN booths as well as the arts and craft, face painting, and manicure stations. Thank you to Jennifer Li, one of our Board of Directors, and to Sherry Meng, our Director of South Bay Enrichment Programs, for help at the FCSN booth. This event could not have been so successful without this group of wonderful people.

We hope FCSN will continue to have similar events in the future. These events help bring Asian families with special needs loved ones closer together as well as educate them on the services that Regional Centers can provide. We want to empower families to advocate for their own children so their children can have access to services that will help them live a fulfilling life within their community.

# AFTER SCHOOL PROGRAM KEEPS FCSN CLIENTS ACTIVE

Mallory Ensminger and Johnna Laird
(FCSN Dream Builders Reporters), Dec 2017

On any weekday mid-afternoon when many children find themselves sitting in front of television, students in FCSN's afterschool program are actively engaged in learning, exercising, and building friendships.

Each afternoon, FCSN's After-school Program emphasizes a different skill, giving participants who can range in age from 5 to 22 an opportunity to explore cooking, arts and crafts, life skills, music, and dance, among other focus areas.

Miss Xiao Yan, head teacher and program coordinator, believes in keeping the program lively. On a particular Thursday in December, participants enjoy a warm afternoon exercising outdoors, then inside where they expect to work on friendship skills. But no! Miss Yan surprises them with a fire drill, an essential skill to understand how to respond calmly in an emergency.

Back inside New Hope Community Church's vestibule-home in Fremont to FCSN's East Bay After-school Program – each of the 13 students present that day retrieve a folding chair, set it up and create a semi-circle where they first stand to play Simon Says, amid laughter and friendly competition. Then Miss Yan leads a discussion about the importance of listening at school and at home. A fun, animated video of a rabbit character that fails to listen brings focused attention with eyes on the screen. After a discussion where children and young adults point out where the character made mistakes, Miss Yan engages students in role plays. Students break out in laughter as they watch volunteers exaggerate behaviors to demonstrate how not to respond in social situations and then show well-received social responses. Students raise their hands to list positive ways to interact with others and ways to show they are listening.

The lesson ends with participants proudly pasting behavior stars on a board, stars to earn credit for a shopping spree before the new year.

In the blink of an eye, Miss Yan is introducing a guest speaker, a teen volunteer with containers of Legos impressing them with a Lego vehicle, powered by a rubber band that flies across and nearly off the table. Soon everyone is gathered around the table, hands-on, digging into the containers and assembling Legos.

FCSN's program is somewhat unique, serving a wide age group that creates community and where individuals encourage and support each other. Program coordinator Yan works with a team of 10 adults, including Kelly Ko, who oversees the program and whose son attended the program for five years.

Operating from 3 to 6 p.m., the program offers a one-to-three ratio, with one adult for every three students. Youth volunteers assist with activities which often make the program seem like one-on-one.

According to Kelly, there are several reasons parents choose FCSN's East Bay After-school Program. First, it provides structure. Instead of going home and experiencing boredom, children at FCSN's After-school Program work on various skills that engage them. Parents can rely on FCSN to provide a safe environment where children are well-cared for during program hours. FCSN offers an educational environment that caters to the needs of each individual child. Most importantly, the adults who operate the program really enjoy children, helping them grow and reach their potential.

Parents of special needs children often experience difficulty in locating a place that meets both educational and social needs, says Kelly. FCSN's after-school program strives to keep students engaged and teach them life skills that can make the rest of their life a bit easier. As a result, new classes are added each year based on what most benefits students who are enrolled.

The week begins with a focus on cooking where students help prepare a meal that is shared with the group. Arts and crafts happen Tuesdays where students make decorations for holidays and special occasions to share with their families. The remainder of the week, students work on life skills, academic enrichment, exercise, and most importantly, fun.

FCSN is continuing to recruit program volunteers who have an interest in getting to know and want the rewarding experience of working with a special needs child.

# FRIENDS COFFEE & TEA WINS INNOVATION AWARD

## James Chiao (FCSN co-president), June 2018

On Nov 4, 2017, FCSN's "Friends Coffee & Tea" received an Innovation Award at the 19th Annual Service Above Self Awards Dinner. The award came from SACR (San Andreas Regional Center) and recognized our approach to provide job training opportunities for people with special needs. We were a bit surprised at the early arrival of the award because the coffee shop was still in the training phase.

The idea of creating a coffee shop first came up in the design committee meetings for the South Bay Center in 2014. The Bascom Center is a commercial property with 8000 square feet, which is significantly larger than our Fremont Center facility. The additional space provided us the luxury of adding a store to provide job training opportunities. Actually, operating a store is not entirely a new idea at FCSN. Back in 2004, FCSN opened a small gift shop, "FCSN Booth," in West San Jose. The "FCSN Booth" doubled as a training site for our clients. Even though the "FCSN Booth" closed a few years later, it gave us confidence that a store can work together with our adult day program.

In 2015 after we decided to operate the store space at the Bascom Center as a coffee shop, we set up a coffee shop team to create a more detailed design. For the interior design, we were fortunate to have the service of Mandy Chang, a principal designer of MGI Interior Design. She volunteered many hours and designed everything from the floor tile to the color of the ceiling. The construction of the Bascom Center was completed at the end of 2016, and the Center opened its doors in March 2017. However, the coffee shop remained only a shell and needed a lot of work.

We also received help from the business side. Vivian Chung, manager of our South Bay Day Program, connected us with SoDoI Coffee, a well-established Berkeley coffee shop. The CEO, Jae Chung, shared his experience with us and taught us not only how to make coffee but also how to run the business. As a result of his help, we now serve SoDoI coffee at our coffee shop. The coffee shop team was also in need of a manager. That's when we approached Roxana, parent of a special needs adult and a part-time FCSN staff member. It turns out that Roxana has an interest in culinary arts, having once written a thesis about a coffee shop business – in other words, she was a perfect fit for the job. In turn, Roxana recruited other staff and volunteers to join the team. Her team decided on the menu, finished the decor, and finalized all the operational details, working with Vivian to define the training program.

We have all heard that it is not easy to run a small business, such as Friends Coffee & Tea. The fact was laid bare when the cafe across the street from the Bascom Center closed its doors last year. Yet we know we are not here to compete with Starbucks or even to make much of a profit. With our coffee shop's "soft opening" in February 2018, we simply wanted to provide a unique place for people to enjoy a good cup of coffee, and at the same time learn a little bit about people with special needs.

**Grand Opening of FCSN's Friends Coffee & Tea (2018)**

# FRIENDS COFFEE & TEA

## Vivian Chiang (FCSN Dream Builder Reporter), June 2018

### *Provides Employment Opportunities for Special Needs*

**Roxana Chiu, store manager of Friends Coffee & Tea**

The first thing you see when you enter Friends Coffee & Tea is a smiling cashier, waiting to take your order. Behind her, a few special needs clients are busy working, preparing coffee and tea or taking a freshly baked croissant out of the oven. To the far right, a brightly lit display of pottery, soaps, and LEGO candy dispensers cover the two walls, advertising endless talents of FCSN's students. Friends Coffee & Tea shop opened unofficially early this year; it was already bustling with customers sipping coffee and conversing with the clients, busy at work, prior to the shop's grand opening in April.

Auntie Roxana Chiu became involved in the making of the coffee shop in September 2016. Auntie Roxana, involved with FCSN for more than seven years, teaches the kids and organizes bus trips for families. She is the parent of a special needs adult as well, so she understands this different and exciting opportunity for the special needs children to showcase their skill sets.

As an avid baker and coffee drinker herself, Auntie Roxana was excited to put her creativity to work. She carefully crafted the menu for the shop, with all the drinks unique, one of a kind. "I just know which one has the right taste, so I just do it," explains Auntie Roxana about her ability to create delicious drinks and baked goods.

Besides the menu, Auntie Roxana and her team designed everything from the logo to the mission statement to the shop name. However, since she's never operated a business before, Auntie Roxana gathered inspiration and advice from many sources. For a coffee shop, the most important resource is the coffee beans. Fortunately, the local, freshly-roasted coffee bean company, SoDoI Coffee, graciously provided coffee beans for FCSN. The coffee company offered Auntie Roxana and her team consultation on hardware and physical machines needed for the shop.

The coffee shop offers a skill training site for the Adult Day Program at FCSN. Clients started training a couple of months prior to the shop opening, learning everything from measuring with teaspoons to taking orders to cleaning the shop. Much of the shop equipment accommodates special needs clients. For example, unlike traditional coffee shops that use high pressurized espresso machines, Friends Coffee & Tea uses freshly brewed coffee so it is easier for clients to access the machines. The recipe for drinks was also revised to allow clients to be comfortable while maintaining drink quality. Auntie

Roxana understands the challenge that teachers and special needs clients face as they train since clients need more practice to remember all the steps and procedures to serve the public.

"Even though you teach them right now, they forget the next step," Auntie Roxana said. "It's very difficult for them – something that we take for granted, but in their [head] it's not [easy]."

Friends Coffee & Tea is a community for all FCSN students to gather and participate – not just for the coffee shop team who takes orders, makes the drinks, and cleans the shop. Many of the ingredients in the drinks, such as mint, are grown in the garden next to the FCSN center, which the gardening group maintains and assists the shop by picking fresh mint leaves. Displays on the walls showcase the wide range of talents FCSN students possess.

Auntie Roxana smiles as she imagines the different events that can be held in the coffee shop. "Probably later on, we'll have Saturday Jazz Time," Auntie Roxana said. "All the kids who can play music can sign up and have five minutes to play some music."

Auntie Roxana emphasizes that the main purpose of the shop is to offer a skill training site for FCSN students. The Adult Day Program coffee shop team works from 10 a.m. to noon, Monday through Thursday. But at other times, the coffee shop is open for all other FCSN students to come help and learn new skill sets.

Ultimately, Auntie Roxana wants Friends Coffee & Tea to attract customers not only because the shop has a special needs label, but also because of its delicious tasting drinks and friendly service.

"Other than supporting FCSN, I wish our customers would visit our coffee shop again and again because of our irresistible, tasty drinks," Auntie Roxana said. "We want to express a big appreciation for people who support FCSN and our dreams, but honestly speaking, a tasty drink usually is the main factor to keep our customers coming back again and again."

Check out the website, stop by, and bring a friend!

# LIVING MORE INDEPENDENTLY WITH FCSN SERVICES

Claudia G. Pina Paz (East Bay Living Service Program Manager) & Nayeli Toto (East Bay Program Director), June 2018

Moving out on your own is a hard process for anyone. There are so many skills to learn, bills to pay, and, most importantly, so many changes to face. It is such a huge milestone in an adult's life, and many times we do not realize how much preparation it truly involves.

FCSN's Independent Living Service (ILS) is highly individualized and developed around the specific needs and goals of each individual. ILS provides individuals with functional-skill training to assist them in achieving greater independence while living in the home of a parent, family member, or other person. ILS helps with the anticipation of what is to come, gaining knowledge and experience in all aspects of life and the assurance of receiving the needed support to successfully transition into a home of one's own. During ILS training, individuals experience working 1:1, hand-by-hand with a trainer to gain experience in the many skills needed for living independently. Individuals practice how to plan for meals, make purchases, take public transportation, set up appointments, manage their health, keep a clean and organized space, care for their own hygiene, and every other skill needed to stay healthy, happy, and safe.

Besides ILS, FCSN also offers Supported Living Services (SLS). SLS is a concept, which creates opportunities for people to choose where they live, with whom they live, and how they lead their lives. Clients learn to build their own space, create relationships, learn skills, and grow in independence daily. Every day at SLS is a new learning opportunity for a client to experience a sense of accomplishment, whether by chopping vegetables for the first time or learning to measure detergent for laundry day. Clients experience life in independence with all the supports and training needed.

FCSN Living Services is rooted in the belief that all persons are entitled to live their lives with dignity and respect and should be supported as a valuable, contributing, productive, and accepted member of the community. FCSN Living Services focuses primarily on interdependence, encouraging and supporting its clients to integrate with their non-disabled peers in the community through recreational/leisure, vocational experiences, and educational fields.

FCSN Living Services focuses on independence in self-care; health and medication management; problem solving; use of community transportation and facilities; behavioral, emotional, cognitive, communication and interpersonal skills. Person-centered planning and self-advocacy are encouraged and supported in all environments.

# A TRAILBLAZER FOR SPECIAL NEEDS: SALLY WU

Helen Chou (FCSN parent and Dream Builders Reporter),
Jan 2019

Today's parents have options for extracurricular activities for their special needs children. FCSN provides sports classes such as swimming, golf, and badminton; there's even Chinese school, Zumba, and art classes readily available for kids of different abilities. These types of programs would not have been easily accessible, if not for the persistence and ingenuity of one parent of a special needs kid.

Thirteen years ago, Sally Wu was looking for swimming classes that would be a good fit for her eight-year-old son Michael, but none of the programs in the area accepted him. Insisting that swimming was an important life skill, Sally enrolled Michael in private lessons at ClubSport Fremont. After two years of taking private lessons from

ClubSport Swimming Director Mark Carter, Michael learned to swim. Encouraged by the results, Sally talked to Mark about starting a swimming camp for special needs kids during the summer months, giving more kids the opportunity to learn this valuable life skill. During the summer of 2005, FCSN swimming summer camp was created with less than ten kids who received one-on-one swimming lessons with trained coaches. Every year since, the camp has grown in popularity; this past summer, the program served more than 70 special needs children.

Since establishing the swimming camp, Sally started several more programs to benefit countless children with special needs. In the interview below, Sally shares some of her experiences starting these programs.

Q: Can you please share what circumstances prompted you to create these programs?

A: The main purpose of these programs is to create opportunities for our special needs kids to explore different aspects of the world. I believe that by helping our kids explore their interests, they can obtain valuable life skills, and we can help them realize their maximum potential.

When Michael was little, I wanted him to try different activities, but I couldn't find programs that were willing to accept special needs kids. I still remember trying to enroll my son at swimming camp when he was eight years old but not being able to find any programs that would accept him. I felt so frustrated and discouraged. Eventually, I talked to Mark at ClubSport about creating a swimming camp especially for special needs kids. He helped me start the camp and provided one-on-one coaches for our kids.

I established the Chinese School from a similar situation. When Michael was also eight years old, I tried really hard to enroll him in Chinese school, but no school would accept him. I then gave up teaching him Chinese and just focused on his English. But when he turned 13, I was surprised that Michael started listening to Chinese songs and began singing Jay Chou's songs every day! I started to regret my decision to not continue to pursue his Chinese education. However, I knew that the existing Chinese schools were not willing to accept him, and even if they did, he would have had to start from kindergarten. So, I thought I should start a school on my own for children with special needs. I started to look for Chinese teachers and students who were interested in learning Chinese.

In 2013, we started our Special Shine Chinese School with only four students. In the first two years, we spent a lot of money on Chinese textbooks shipped from Taiwan. I worried that the program would not attract enough students to continue, so I started looking for funding. In 2015, I registered with the Special Shine Chinese School with the Ministry of Education in Taiwan and received free Chinese textbooks from the Taipei Economic and Cultural Representative Office (TECO). We also received funding from World Bright Special Shine (WBSS) Way Inc., which is instrumental in providing funds to help us expand our program to also include art and dance classes.

Q: Were there challenges that you encountered along the way?

A: It was very challenging to establish the program and the school at first. I did not have the resources, and my specialty was not in education. In the beginning, I spent a lot of time researching, organizing, and exploring different resources that might benefit our kids. After the first year, the programs started to gain traction and run more smoothly as other parents began to participate more.

One major challenge that we always have is that we are always short on experienced volunteers for the sports programs and for Chinese school. Another challenge I often deal with is parents' anxiety regarding their kids. While I understand this desire to protect our kids, we want to let the teachers and volunteers handle the students' activities and for students to learn to listen to the teachers and helpers, so we do not let parents sit in on classes in Chinese school. The only programs that include parent participation are Zumba and golf. We also face the challenge of needing more space to run these classes as our programs expand.

Sometimes, I feel tired because of my busy schedule, but just seeing the smile on the faces of the kids and seeing their potential for growth keeps me going. Right now, Emily Lin helps me as administrator of the Chinese School, which makes things easier for me. As the programs grow, I think that we need to start training the next generation of program coordinators to keep continuing the program.

Q: What do you envision for these programs?

A: I feel very positive about these programs because I can see our kids' growth in so many different ways. Some students improve on their drawing. Some students can sit at the table without behavior. I feel so happy when I see that they improve their skills and behaviors through these programs. I love to see kids explore their talents, and I feel most empowered when I see them smiling and enjoying the programs. I think that is the main motivation to keep me going.

Q: What advice do you have for parents who have kids whose needs are not being met by existing programs?

A: I would advise parents to try to create opportunities for their kids. We are the first line to provide our kids with the best opportunities and environments to help them with their disabilities. I believe that with caring, patience, and love, every parent can make it happen.

I look for programs that will benefit my own child first; if there are no programs that are suitable, then I create a program for it. When I started the Golf Program, I didn't know anyone who played golf. I went to the Fremont Golf Course near Mission and Stevenson and talked to the owner, Alex Jansen, and told him my concept of pairing special needs kids with their own parents to manage their behaviors. I needed a paid coach to give them instructions, and I also wanted to find funding to decrease the financial burden on the parents.

Also, after a child becomes interested in a particular activity, parents can help them succeed by moving them toward private lessons to obtain more advanced skills. One of the children in our programs, Austin, is very good at ceramics. Austin started off with my son, Michael, in a small one-on-two class with a private teacher in his ceramics studio. We could see that Austin truly enjoyed and excelled at ceramics, so his mom sought to expand his skill through more classes. Now, Austin's ceramic pieces are sold at South Bay's FCSN Friends Coffee & Tea. Our programs can provide opportunities and open the door to discover our kids' talents, but once that talent is discovered, parents should help them maximize their potential by seeking further opportunities.

Of course, we have many people in the community who support us and help make these programs possible, like Mark and the management team at ClubSport, and Alex Jansen, the owner of the Fremont Golf Course. Anna Wang and Sylvia Yeh of FCSN help us apply for and obtain grants to support our programs, and we are so lucky to have the support of WBSS Way Inc. to keep our programs and Chinese School running. Also, with parents' support, we can make the programs run longer and expand to other areas.

Q: What advice can you give to parents of special needs individuals?

A: Never give up. Keep trying to discover your kid's talents and interests. I still remember my son cried and screamed for almost two years when I enrolled him in swimming. His behavior was so challenging that none of the coaches could handle him. I struggled with the decision, but I did not give up, and I insisted that he needed to learn to swim. At that time, I did not see swimming as just a sport, but rather I treated it as a vital life skill. I talked to Mark, the swimming director at ClubSport, who decided to teach my son himself. After the initial struggle, it turned out that my son LOVED to swim. I will never forget his smiling face when he was swimming in the pool. He now knows all the different strokes and really enjoys it.

In some cases, it may be that the kids are not quite ready to explore a certain skill at that time. One child in Chinese School had a very hard time the first year and withdrew from the program after a couple of classes. However, by the next year, the parents decided to give it another try; this time the kid was ready. He was happy to join in on activities, and he really loved the classes. So, my advice to parents is "Never give up on your kids."

# SEP & TDS: ROADMAP TO EMPLOYMENT

## Claire Go (SEP Manager), Jan 2019

**High Five to Shannon's first paycheck.**

Believing that people with special needs can be successful members of the workforce if given opportunities, support, and training, FCSN established Supported Employment Program (SEP) in East Bay in September 2017 and in the South Bay in October 2018 to help clients reach their employment goals.

A small, yet dedicated, SEP team works extremely hard to not only locate possible employment opportunities but also to provide pre-employment training for clients who express interest in finding employment. It is with great pride to share that we have successfully placed fourteen clients in competitive employment in East Bay within a year! This is a great accomplishment for FCSN and clients, considering all the hours our SEP team put into training, job searches, job applications and job coaching to ensure employment and retention.

When we first started, I had doubts about how receptive business owners would be toward hiring our clients. I was pleasantly surprised! With the support of kind-hearted people and businesses that promote inclusion, individuals with special needs are finally getting the chance to be truly integrated in the community.

Aside from SEP, we also recently started our Tailored Day Service (TDS) Program, which is aimed at serving clients who won't typically fit in a day program setting. TDS is a very individualized program consisting of a maximum of six hours per week supporting clients in their personal and employment goals. Through TDS, we are able to develop and provide in-depth, hands-on pre-employment training. We currently have fifteen TDS clients in the East Bay, six of whom have found employment. We already have referrals for our South Bay TDS which will start in early 2019.

It has been a very hectic year for our Supported Employment Program and Tailored Day Service, but looking at where we are now, I can safely say that it is worth it. Our clients are worth it.

GO SEP! GO TDS!

# FCSN OVERCOMES CHALLENGES FOR CLIENTS TO TAKE COLLEGE COURSES

## Johnna Laird (FCSN Dream Builders Reporter), Dec 2019

Special Needs, Eastbay Day Program Manager Vivian "Wei Wei" Largusa culminated two years of hard work to enroll seven FCSN clients at Ohlone Community College on the Fremont campus.

Limited hours when clients were available during FCSN's Day Program and Ohlone's regulations posed challenges that at times seemed insurmountable.

"For the past two years I have been in contact with individuals from Ohlone where we were trying to figure out a way for our clients to take courses. Courses offered during the allotted times for clients to attend turned out to be courses that some clients had already taken," said Wei Wei, explaining part of the challenge. Plus, the college has new regulations limiting the number of times that students can enroll in classes, and no exceptions are made for students with special needs.

When FCSN surveyed clients, a number of new clients expressed interest in enrolling in classes even with few offerings. Exercise classes received the greatest interest among courses.

Beyond the hurdles posed within Ohlone's regulations, FCSN encountered slow responses from clients and families. "It was difficult in some cases getting commitments from families and clients. Sometimes clients were interested, but we did not receive timely responses back from families," said Wei Wei.

The seven students enrolled in a cardio class, integrated with other students and without any modifications.

The cardio class is the first of what Wei Wei intends to be an on-going program of enrolling FCSN clients in Ohlone College courses.

"Our clients who are attending are very proud and excited to be taking Ohlone classes. They have already been talking about what courses they may want to enroll in next semester," says Wei Wei. Another challenge, she adds, is finding similar classes that interest clients.

"I love it," says Diane, one of the participants. "It gives me a chance to lose weight and increase my heart rate. The coach has helped a lot using weights." Meghan is equally enthusiastic: "It's awesome learning things. I'm getting muscles and it's helping me get into a dress for the wedding," where she is a bridesmaid. "There are lots of tests, but they are okay."

"It's nice to be around other people on the college campus," says Kendra, who likes the variety of participating in the Tuesday-Thursday cardio class from 11 a.m. to 12:30. "I like the teacher. He is really nice. He wants everyone to pass and earn an A. I got five out of five on one quiz and four out of five on another. We do weights and the treadmill and the bike. He teaches how to build more muscle and lose weight. Some stretches are good. I think they are improving my balance."

As long as there's sufficient client interest shown in taking courses, Wei Wei plans to continue courses at Ohlone. Client interest will determine the type of courses chosen. "We need at least four clients to sign up for a course to have at least one group for the class," she says. "We need four clients to justify the expense of having one staff member present with them in the class. The staff member is there to assist clients, encourage, help understand directions and assist with any necessary modifications.

"We also want to consider classes that may not require outside course work as our staff will not always be available to support clients with homework," she explains.

# FULLY INTEGRATING INTO LOCAL COMMUNITIES

Vivian Chung (FCSN South Bay Program Director), Dec 2019

FCSN W.I.L.L. (WORK, INTEGRATE, LEARN, LIVE) Adult Day Program in San Jose offers a variety of innovative skill training for clients to learn computer skills, practice healthy lifestyles and independent living skills, engage in prevocational training, and participate in life-enrichment clubs. FCSN also arranges community outings for clients to choose from, based on their interests and preferences. Community involvement includes Timpany Aqua Aerobic, San Jose City College, local parks, and museums, among others.

To offer a variety of volunteer experiences for clients to choose from, FCSN diligently establishes collaborations and partnerships with the community that include: Meals on Wheels, the Girl Scout Office, community centers, City of Campbell Parks, and many more. FCSN clients participate in schedule planning with their support staff and choose what they want to do.

FCSN clients and staff have made great differences to the community through volunteering. For example, FCSN has participated in the Meals on Wheels Program since 2010. FCSN clients deliver hot, nutritious meals two days a week to seniors and adults with disabilities. In addition to meals, FCSN clients and staff also provide daily wellness checks, making sure that seniors and disabled individuals are safe, alert and cared for. FCSN also partners with Tzu Chi Foundation where volunteers prepared toiletries for senior care facility victims of Woolsey Fire.

For more than a year FCSN clients have generated in excess of 1800 hours at Campbell Park Projects. Their abilities surprised a lot of people. With support from the FCSN staff, not only did clients help beautify local parks, they participated in special projects like repairing picnic tables and benches. They sanded and painted new planks of wood and assembled them together. Some parents told me that they were very surprised to see their adult children being so capable using electric drills and tools. One of the most rewarding moments for our clients was their invitation to the City of Campbell's Volunteer Luncheon on May 1, 2019, and receiving recognition for outstanding volunteer work! Our clients told others how proud they were being invited and took lots of selfies. They were very excited! FCSN filled two tables at the luncheon!

Besides devoted volunteer work, FCSN clients also truly integrate into the community. For example, a group of four clients along with a staff member volunteer at Mayfair Community Center to stuff event fliers into monthly activity catalogs, organize a storage room, and clean gym equipment.

They are welcomed to join classes Mayfair Community Center hosts. Earlier this year, our clients proudly received volunteer recognitions from State Senator Jim Beall. Through fruitful volunteer work and integration in the community, FCSN clients give their talents, become productive, build self-confidence, make new friends, create meaningful lives and gain happiness as contributing community members.

Two years in a row, FCSN Percussion Ensemble and FCSN musicians have been invited to perform at Make Music Day hosted by Bascom Community Center along with other community music groups. They have performed, enjoyed music of other groups, and had a great time dancing. This is another inclusion experience where FCSN clients come as equal, community partners.

Deepest appreciation goes to the supportive community partners, parents, FCSN's diligent staff and clients for creating another fruitful year for FCSN's South Bay Adult Day Program.

# PRESIDENT'S MESSAGE 2019

## CK Lee (Co-President 2018-2019), June 2019

For the past eleven months, I have had the honor of being FCSN's co-president. It's been a good opportunity for me to fully understand the FCSN operation. We can divide the FCSN operation into two portions, the family side and the business side. Since most FCSN members are familiar with the family side, I will talk a little more about the business side.

FCSN receives funding from the regional centers, allowing us to hire staff to operate our adult day program, living services, supported employment, and more. FCSN is blessed to have so many dedicated and hardworking staff members. They do an excellent job helping our children lead fruitful and meaningful lives. However, the living cost in the Bay Area is so high, and state funding is limited, so we are constantly looking for more staff. Currently we have almost twenty open positions, so please spread the word that FCSN is hiring. You can check our website, www.fcsn1996.org for more details.

FCSN has been an organization for twenty-three years, and when I became co-president, I found that we had needs for a technology upgrade, so we worked a lot on those aspects. We have improved and added online registration, a volunteer management system, a member database, a client management system, and more. Our team worked very hard to make these systems run efficiently, and we would love for everyone to use them. We ask that you please switch to the new systems as much as you can. Thank you.

Finally, I'd like to emphasize the importance of participation. Every month we host a coffee social, an afternoon tea social, and a parents' lunch (friendship forever). Even if you aren't able to attend our enrichment programs with your children, please consider joining us at our parents' social events once in a while because FCSN is here to serve every family member, and with your participation our children will have a brighter future.

# CHAPTER 7:
# The Pandemic Years
## *(2020-2021)*

In January 2020, we started to hear about COVID-19, a disease that seemed foreign and distant from us. However, in March, Governor Newson announced "Shelter in Place" order; suddenly, the dark cloud of COVID-19 was upon us: all FCSN in-person events were canceled, and all in-person programs postponed except for essential services. While every family was experiencing some difficulties, FCSN was facing unprecedented challenges. Under president CK Lee's leadership, the management team (Sylvia Yeh, Anna Wang, Lilian Lin and their key staff) has done an incredible job in managing this crisis.

Under immense pressure, our team of staff and volunteers have responded with many virtual and online programs to support our clients and children who are now staying at home. Not only that many old programs were converted to online format, but there were also a host of new virtual programs – reaching out not only to nearby clients and members, but also to new individuals far away from our centers. The spirit of corporation and the sense of community was nothing we have seen since the Dream Project days.

And finally, as more people have been vaccinated and the situation gets under control, FCSN is preparing for the gradual re-opening of our in-person programs in the second half of 2021.

# PRESIDENT'S MESSAGE 2020

## CK Lee (President 2019-2020), June 2020

| Sample Schedule | Monday | Tuesday | Wednesday | Thursday | Friday |
|---|---|---|---|---|---|
| 10:00 – 10:45 | ZUMBA | Dance | Stretching | Yoga | Sing Along |
| 11:00 – 11:45 | Current Event | Math | Tasty Recipes | Personal Hygiene | Virtual Tours |
| 11:45 – 12:15 | Social Time/ Virtual Lunch | | | | |
| 12:15 – 1:00 | Life Skills | Game Time | It's story TiME | Social Skills | Show & Tell |
| 1:15 – 2:00 | Science | Arts & Crafts | Reading | COVID-19 Prevention | Weekly Recap |

Dear FCSN Families and Friends,

I would like to give you the FCSN annual report via newsletter during this challenging time. My wish is that you and your family are doing well. My hope is that everyone stays safe.

Since 2019, FCSN has been working on technology upgrades which include both hardware and software. You may have noticed that some of FCSN's programs now use online registration instead of paper forms. The volunteer management system helps FCSN communicate better with all the volunteers. The member database and human resource information system (HRIS) helps internal management tremendously. Currently we are working on a client management system, cybersecurity, and our website. These enhancements require resources to support them, and we appreciate all the help from our donors, volunteers, and board so that we can continue to make FCSN better.

FCSN has been an organization for twenty-four years, and we have grown to over 1000 family members. Unfortunately, some families drift away for various reasons. In the past year we have tried very hard to connect with more members because we want to hear from them to see how we can better serve our members' needs. We have held a monthly "friendship forever" parent lunch meeting, and we also have held a full-day core member meeting. From these meetings we have strengthened our connection with members and explained the operational challenges to clear up any misunderstandings. We also have realized that it is impossible for FCSN to fulfill everyone's needs due to limited resources, so we must be creative and think outside the box. Currently we are communicating with other vendors to see if we can better serve our members with a collaboration. We've met a director from Trumpet Behavior Company to see if this entity can train our staff, so that our staff knows how to better serve our clients with behavior challenges. We will also invite the LSA executive director to talk about their group home living services since not all members' loved ones are able to utilize supported living. These are all on-going efforts, and if you know of any good vendors, please introduce them to us, too.

FCSN has held an annual gala fundraising event since 2002, and the gala format and $100 ticket price has not changed for seventeen years; however, the total cost of each participant is now much more than $100, so we had to make some changes in 2019. After some discussion, the gala committee decided to raise the ticket price to $200 and reduce the number of guests to 350. This was a big change as we've hosted 800 to 1,200 guests in the past years. Many members also brought up concerns that the ticket price was too high. In the past years the gala has served multiple purposes including fundraising, member reunion, and our special kids' performances, but starting from 2019 we wanted to shift the focus of the gala and make fundraising the sole purpose. With a clearer goal in mind, we were able to plan this event better. We received a lot of positive feedback and ended up achieving our fundraising goal; we will continue with a similar format in 2020.

Earlier this year, we were preparing to explore some different South Bay after school programs. Unfortunately, we encountered the coronavirus outbreak in early March, and many members suggested stopping all programs to protect our children, especially because many special needs persons are most at-risk. We halted enrichment programs and family gatherings from the first week of March but kept vendored programs at that time since they were funded by the regional center. Stopping those programs would have required regional center approval. When the San Francisco Bay Area shelter-in-place order took effect on March 16th, FCSN stopped all vendored programs except for essential services. We understand that this is a tough time for everyone, and we want to take care of our staff as much as we can, even if we cannot hold our regular programs in person. Therefore, Albert, Anna, Sylvia, Lilian, and I have decided that most of our staff (excluding coffee shop staff and respite workers) will continue to receive their regular pay. We also want to express our appreciation to our essential workers during this unprecedented period, so the working staff will receive double pay. We are so grateful for everyone's willingness to help. Our staff quickly organized online courses for our clients, so everyone can stay connected with each other remotely. Below is an example of our East Bay Adult Day Program online courses. We are truly blessed to have so many dedicated and wonderful staff members.

This year brings new challenges for us all. Even though FCSN annual meetings will be canceled, we will continue to have volunteer awards, board elections, and the like. Although many things are uncertain, FCSN is ready to face any situation. Let's stay close even if we are apart!

# FCSN REMOTE SERVICES

## Nayeli Toto (East Bay Program Director), June 2020

Ever since "Shelter-In-Place" was enforced on March 17th, FCSN has faced an unprecedented challenge. Having to temporarily close our doors to many of our programs was a difficult pill to swallow for many of us but even more so for our clients. Sudden routine changes with an abrupt break to their usual rituals and a change of scenery presented rapid alterations, making the situation almost too much to handle. At FCSN, our main mission coupled with our goal has always been to support our clients and their families. During this difficult time especially, our commitment to our community has truly shone brighter than ever.

In less than a week, our dedicated teams created a full spectrum of virtual classes. Day Program, SEP, and Living Services joined forces for planning and program development for classes that their clients needed, wanted and would enjoy. Together we created engaging classes and activities to keep clients' minds engaged and learning while keeping their bodies strong.

Our dozens of classes are tailored to the needs of our different clients and are geared toward their development, their creativity and their needs to stay active. With the support from their families and caregivers, clients are joining classes from their family homes, group homes and from our Supported Living service. Our clients are able to socialize through our structured virtual gatherings while participating in different classes and engaging in giving their feedback. Clients are with their peers and staff; they learn and play, benefitting from physical activity and pure fun.

Thanks to these innovative and creative classes, we have seen the worried and confused faces of our clients switch to happier and confident ones. Parents saw the change, too. "I was so impressed by the number of clients who attended," "The class was well-organized (good music)!" "My daughter had a great time! I'm sure other clients are feeling the same, too." "Looking forward to the next Zumba class," "FCSN teams are superheroes during this pandemic"

We know connection is everything for our clients. We are part of their village, and being able to show them our love and support while also teaching and engaging them to have fun is our privilege.

# BRINGING FRIENDS OF CHILDREN TO THE VIRTUAL WORLD

Jake Haw (FCSN South Bay W.I.L.L. Adult Day Program Coordinator), June 2020

The Bay Area was hit really hard with the arrival of the global pandemic to the United States. California's governor issued a Shelter-in-Place order, forcing everyone to stay in their own homes for safety. What did this mean for clients who attend FCSN's Day Program regularly? Responding immediately, FCSN's different management teams and all staff discussed and collaborated on a solution to this: Virtual classes served as the Day Program for those sheltering in place.

Each week of classes start by allotting time for greetings and checking-in on the clients to see how they are doing and if they want to share anything interesting from their day or weekend. Some days, instructors create a theme to generate extra enthusiasm, such as Hat Day, when clients wear favorite hats, showing a bit more of their personalities, or share a favorite book for "Book Day." Excitement and smiles abound as clients share their items during the week. Classes also include physical fitness, social development, and academic excellence, as well as some creativity classes.

FCSN instructors prepare different exercises throughout the day to create variety. For physical fitness, clients enjoy Zumba with teacher Hanh on Monday; Yoga with teachers Jake and Ramona on Tuesday; Stretching and Nutrition with teachers Jeffrey and Phyllis on Wednesdays; Aerobics with teachers Kim and Darlynn on Thursdays; and Stability & Exercise with teachers Michael and Corinna on Fridays. Every day, clients sweat some as they exercise through dancing, stretching, and doing cardio exercises that really engage their bodies. Not only do clients love it, but some of their parents join in and love it, too. These activities encourage clients to maintain their physical health and participate together and enjoy.

For social development, teachers Phyllis and Jeffrey offer Social Stories class, focusing on important social skills like ways to deal with strangers, using polite words and manners, what to do when lost, working together as a team, among many more skills. Clients participate and learn through watching videos, participating in question-and-answer segments, giving their own examples, and singing a song to end the class. Clients say that they enjoy learning social skills through this fun class.

FCSN continues to offer classes in Reading and Money Management, plus a new class to inform clients about the novel coronavirus. Classes are taught with a smaller ratio, four clients to one instructor. This allows for a more focused discussion to enhance learning, based on client skill level, which enhances interest and focus to maximize learning. Clients have shared that these smaller classes make participation easier for them. They give these classes two thumbs up!

Known for bringing out client creativity, FCSN offers a spectrum of classes to meet client needs: Body Percussion class with teachers Po, Stanley, and Jeffrey; Performing Arts with teachers Phyllis and Corinna; Cooking with teacher Darlynn, Kim, Casie, and Ramona; Arts and Crafts with teacher Emily, Ann, Darlynn, and Corinna; and Games with teachers Jake and Emily. Classes are designed so clients can use resources they have at home.

To simulate FCSN Day Program's lunchtime that offers clients time for interaction, teachers created a virtual lunch daily at noon. Clients share just as they would at the Day Program, using the time to eat and talk about food, sharing stories about their lives as friends do. Interestingly, clients practice cleaning up and washing their plates and utensil after they eat, practicing self-care and independence in a safe environment. Clients even check up on each other and remind each other to get ready for the next class.

Special Clubs offer a variety of topics, everything from travel to movies to music. In the future special clubs will expand to include photography, beauty for ladies and a mirror club for the gentlemen. Not only do these clubs offer interesting topics to prompt discussion, they also enhance client engagement and focus as clients participate in distance learning classes in the Virtual Day Program. The pandemic has shown that FCSN clients, like students in elementary, middle, high school and college, can actively learn through remote classes.

# FCSN'S VIRTUAL LEARNING PROGRAMS

Mannching Wang (FCSN Youth Volunteer Coordinator),
Oct. 6, 2020

When FCSN temporarily closed its programs to comply with Sheltering in Place for safety to prevent the spread of the coronavirus in the San Francisco Bay Area, I was glad to hear that our FCSN volunteers wanted to continue teaching programs to our children.

Jacob Wang and his team, teachers of South Bay Family Gathering (SBRG) percussion class, were the first volunteer group to reach out to me about their intention to continue the percussion class virtually.

I discussed this proposal with the SBRG program coordinator and Linmei Chiao, head of FCSN's Volunteer Support Team, and decided this would be a great idea using online video. Fortunately, the volunteer teachers of the art class and the movement class also expressed interest in continued teaching through videos.

I provided guidelines to the volunteer teachers for virtual teaching. For example, the instructors should greet students at the beginning of the video, followed by showing their students what they planned to teach in the video and providing students with a list of materials required. I recommended teachers choose easily available project materials that students could find in their homes. I also recommended that instructors go step-by-step for each skill at a pace suitable for our special needs students. At the end of the teaching video, I recommended the volunteer teachers say goodbye and praise the students.

After SBRG virtual classes were established, I continued to recruit from FCSN's volunteer database for teachers interested in creating a class and teaching virtually. Volunteers stepped up and created drawing and story-reading classes for all FCSN students.

Linmei encouraged me to launch 1:1 virtual teaching. We paired one volunteer with one student, depending upon the student's interest and tailoring the class to the student's individual needs. FCSN now offers 1:1 classes in science, music, drawing, reading, playing games, among others. Parents played a major role in 1:1 classes by training volunteers, preparing teaching materials, and sitting with their children during the 1:1 sessions.

Finally, we tailored a virtual teaching program for students with limited function. We coordinated a small social group with size of five to six students where non-verbal students have higher enrollment priority. Using google meeting, volunteers lead story reading and music activities. Students also participate in fun activities like show and tell.

From my viewpoint, this virtual teaching response created a win-win situation for FCSN family and our youth volunteers as well as our students. Our children got the opportunity to work with a peer not only on a specific subject but also socially interact with regular peers. Our youth volunteers received a great opportunity by learning how to develop a teaching plan, teaching in step-by-step fashion, and modifying their teaching for our special needs children. Years from now, our youth volunteers may look back on this time as an opportunity to learn how to work with our children and bring this experience to the rest of their lives and their community, benefitting the understanding of special needs people.

# FCSN CLUBS

## Isabella He (Youth volunteer
## & FCSN Youth Club coordinator), Jan. 2020

**Zoom meeting in session for our check-in meetings with representatives from each school club attending.**

As the founder and president of the first FCSN club at my high school (Mission San Jose High School), I have seen the great impact that an FCSN club can have. Our club now has 90+ members, with many active members participating in various FCSN programs, even during Shelter-In-Place. As one of our first events, we hosted a training orientation for our members new to FCSN, introducing approximately forty new volunteers to FCSN.

Seeing the impact of the MSJ FCSN Club, FCSN's Director of Volunteer Support Linmei Chiao had the idea of expanding FCSN clubs to high schools and colleges all over the bay area. Since then, we have created a program to mentor/coach volunteers to start their own FCSN clubs with eleven plus new clubs in the making.

## What is the 'FCSN Club at Your School' program?

With experience from my own club formation process, our program provides aspiring club leaders with guidance and mentorship with forming and running their FCSN clubs. Our program hosts bi-weekly meetings to maintain progress on club formation and coordinate activities/events across schools.

Forming an FCSN club helps the community of individuals with special needs in FCSN, beyond FCSN, and also fosters the volunteers' leadership skills.

FCSN school clubs have the following common objectives:

- Promote FCSN programs to students to expand FCSN's impact and recruit volunteers
- Increase awareness and understanding of neurodiversity in schools
- Coordinate volunteer training and other events to students in a scalable way

The club's overarching goal is to support the community of individuals with special needs. All club activities will aim to support this goal.

## What have you learned from this process?

The work that our teams have put in and their dedication to FCSN has been amazing to witness. Teams have drafted up twenty plus pages of club documents, made presentations for club approval, reached out to teachers and school staff for club advisors, gotten hundreds of student signatures, and more, all in the span of a couple of weeks this summer.

It's been inspirational and motivating to see, and I'm excited about the future of this program. Cross-school activities and events will be an exciting avenue to pursue.

## Testimonial from volunteers in this program and leaders of their own FCSN clubs:

"None of the three of us had any experience of forming a new club before, but FCSN has been incredibly supportive that they have Isabella He from MSJ's FCSN club helping us basically every step of the way; we've asked her so many questions that we otherwise wouldn't know where to turn to. We don't see our inexperience as a disadvantage; we feel that it will motivate us to listen, to learn, and to experiment what will work in our own school – and it could actually be a strength of our team…we hope [our school] will be made a few more steps closer to being an inclusive community." – Isabelle Hsu, Sean Lin, and Hannah Wilson from Irvington High School's FCSN Club team

If you are a volunteer interested in joining our program and starting an FCSN club at your own school, please email me.

# FCSN KIDS AND YOUNG ADULTS FIND THEIR VOICES IN TOASTMASTERS

## Dan Rachlin (FCSN parent), Sept. 2020

About two years ago, I attended a routine IEP for my son Sammy. At the beginning of the meeting, his teacher Ms. Louis mentioned that Sammy would be giving his own presentation. I was quietly skeptical, expecting that this would be a very watered-down sort of affair. When it came time for the presentation, Sammy stood up in front of his small audience, and gave a slide presentation describing his progress and expectations. I was amazed at how he was able to do things that I would expect out of a trained speaker. He made very effective eye contact, his voice was strong, and his timing was perfect. It seemed like Sammy was transformed. I was stunned and realized that something profound had happened.

Months later, I reflected on this event and it occurred to me that Toastmasters could be a great match for Special Needs. From where I stood, having one foot in the world of special needs and another in Toastmasters, this fact appeared obvious on many levels. Ms. Louis provided some tips and a few from Saratoga Toastmasters went to work.

It is useful to inject some background about Toastmasters International. The organization was founded in 1924 by Ralph C. Smedley in a YMCA in Santa Ana, California to assist young men in improving their communication skills. The concept progressed and the organization was formally incorporated here in California in 1932. It quickly grew and became an international organization. These days it can be found on all the continents – while there is no club in Antarctica, a speech was recently given there by a past member of Saratoga Toastmasters.

A pilot activity was started in Sept. of 2019 with the purpose of introducing the Toastmasters experience to FCSN individuals with special needs. We benefited greatly from the help of Alan's mother Jennifer Li who had the foresight to obtain a popular time slot during the Saturday evening family gatherings. Our first wave of volunteers comprised members of Saratoga Toastmasters. Other waves of volunteers have participated. This activity could not get off the ground without the efforts of these individuals.

Throughout the fall, we had a successful series of meetings. Attendance was typically twenty-five or more. At first, Toastmasters volunteers played many of the roles. Our young adults gave prepared speeches, but our young adults were wary of other roles such as Toastmaster of the Day. Steadily, as the weeks went by more and more of these roles were filled with young adults.

Everything happily progressed until the Chinese New Year, when FCSN and other entities were shut down due to the COVID-19 response. Toastmasters Clubs locally and throughout the world had to deal with this issue. When our sponsor Gopal suggested we have our meetings online, we had something of a model for how to make this scenario work. We started our Zoom-meetings in March. Instead of bi-weekly, they were weekly, and it was extremely satisfying to see how our members took on the challenge so capably with regular attendance. With only a few diminishing exceptions, roles are filled exclusively by young adults.

Currently we are focused on chartering the club – the process of becoming an officially recognized Toastmasters club. We have about a dozen regular young adults but will need some parents to join to help and to bring the initial count to twenty as required. Becoming a club will allow us to participate in the formal education program of Toastmasters. Members will give speeches much as they do now but following a curriculum wherein each speech will emphasize special-ized objectives. There are online teaching videos and other materials that go with these speech projects. The program is called "Pathways." As a club, we will have officer roles that can be shared by parents and young adults. These include President, VP Education, VP Membership, Secretary and Sergeant at Arms. There are many district level educa-tional events that one can attend. And of course, it is always possible to visit other clubs as a guest to see how they operate. Many will be pleased to note that other clubs operate very much like ours.

As time goes on, we hope to integrate the Special Needs partic-ipation with certain mainstream Toastmasters curriculum elements, better allowing Toastmasters members to get education credit for their volunteer work with us. A good example is one-on-one men-toring – consider how the possibilities have opened now that we are all comfortable with online conferencing. We wish to put ourselves on the map as an FCSN Toastmasters club so that these and other opportunities can come about.

Toastmasters can be, and for many has become, a lifetime activity. In this sense, it compares very well with the Special Olympics. With its world-wide reach, one can take time during travel to visit a local Toastmasters club and be welcomed as if one were at home. If one moves to another location, there is a high likelihood that a Toastmasters club is available locally to join.

One might get this far and still ask, why be concerned with public speaking when simple one-on-one dialog is most often the primary concern? There are many answers to this question. Certainly, the meetings are a source of fun learning with friends. By having a performance dimension, we create focus and thereby a greater sense of accomplishment during each instance of successful communication. Finally, consider leadership – as is developed through taking on meeting roles and officer roles. Being a leader in any situation contributes to one's successful management of other challenges in life. It is therefore understandable that the logo of Toastmasters International, an organization most often associated with communication, includes the tagline "Where Leaders Are Made."

# FCSN VOICES

Isabella He and Ryan Liu (Youth volunteers and
FCSN Voices editors), Dec. 2020

"As soon as our organization was just established in late 1996, we started working on FCSN printed newsletter, and we published the first issue in January 1997," FCSN Co-Chair and FCSN Voices Advisor Jim Chiao said. "The newsletter reported announcements, organizational updates, and articles from parents and volunteers, it helped bring our organization together and grow. Today, twenty-four years later, I see FCSN Voices as a huge extension of FCSN newsletter, with all the power that comes with the digital platform."

FCSN Voices was formerly known as FCSN Blog. The blog started about five to six years ago with the publication of personal stories of our clients in the Adult Day Programs and Living Programs. About three years ago, Jim took over the blog to broaden its scope and reported on the latest news/events from all sectors within FCSN. Then three months ago, our Volunteer Director Linmei Chiao received an email from a youth volunteer Ryan, saying that he could help to make the blog a lot better with more personal and detailed blogs – Jim was very receptive to the idea, and that's how Jim and Ryan first got connected. Two weeks later, our tutoring coordinator of SNTutoring Isabella heard of the news and joined the team. Just around the same time, Jim was talking to Wei-Jen about recruiting youth volunteers for the FCSN printed newsletter, and found out that Helen, an editor, was also interested in bringing our newsletter online. It was amazing the speed that we put this team together; within weeks, we had a good working team. Soon, we were publishing at least one article each week. Now, after many weeks of publishing and discussion, we decided to change the name of the publication and FCSN Voices was born.

The name *FCSN Voices* was chosen to allow the voices of the special needs community to be heard, which consists of special needs individuals, their families and friends, and volunteers and professionals who dedicate their time and effort to improve the lives of special needs individuals. We aim to provide information about FCSN events and programs; inspirational stories about special need individuals; and personal accounts of volunteer initiatives.

> *"As an adult volunteer for FCSN, I hope that FCSN Voices will reach out and touch the hearts of many people and inspire them to become involved with FCSN. By sharing stories, events, and perspectives from our large community, FCSN Voices could provide readers with an idea of the joy and fulfillment one feels from being part of FCSN's welcoming family. I hope it will give potential volunteers some ideas of how they can use their unique skills and voices to support FCSN; for example, by contributing to this publication!"*
>
> *FCSN Voices Advisor, Wei-Jen Hsia*

FCSN Voices publishes at least one new featured article each week. Our team currently consists of five core members and a growing team of volunteer youth reporters. We are open to contributions from all members, staff, and volunteers, as we believe that everyone has a unique story that can make a difference in someone else's life. We are constantly looking for ways to add a fresh voice and a new dimension to our publication to cover a wider scope and serve a much wider audience. We hope this will be an important platform for FCSN to share our dream of building a community for our children & adults with special needs. We look forward to the day when all special needs individuals are fully embraced by the community they live in, becoming an active part of the integrated community. We hope FCSN Voices can play an important role in working towards that goal.

*Follow the FCSN Voices to stay tuned with new stories and events! If you have something to share, please contact our editors.*

## Meet the Team Behind the Scenes:

**Editors:**

Blog Coordinator, Parent Contact – Helen Chou

Youth Reporter Lead, Volunteer Contact – Isabella He

Web Editor, Marketing Manager – Ryan Liu

**Advisors:**

Jim Chiao

Wei-Jen Hsia

**Youth Reporters:**

Nitya, Alice, Hillary, Andria, Anna, Shreya, Kaitlyn, Jessica, Sara, and Daniel

# PRESIDENT'S MESSAGE

## C.K. Lee President 2020-2021, Dec. 2020

Dear FCSN Families and Friends,

I hope you are doing well during this tough time. The COVID-19 pandemic has lasted for almost a year now, and the number of confirmed cases has continued to climb. Even though a vaccine is on its way and beginning to be administered, we may not be back to normal for a while, so please be patient. If you need any support, please contact our family support representative, Dora Chou.

During the past six months, FCSN was able to continue to host our annual events online. We held a virtual annual meeting in June, a special needs talent showcase in August, and a virtual fundraising gala in November. We also have online classes for our adult day program and enrichment program. Our flexible subject tutoring classes have become quite popular, and we have received positive feedback from many families. We may continue this class online after the pandemic, since some students learn better in an online format.

FCSN receives a lot of support from our community, and in turn we try to give back to the community as well. The FCSN board has recently approved an emergency relief fund and a college scholarship fund. FCSN staff and clients in need of financial support may apply for the emergency relief fund. Any college or graduate student whose major is human services-related is eligible to apply for the college scholarship fund, although FCSN volunteers will have priority in receiving the scholarship. These two funds are currently a work in progress and will become available in 2021.

To serve our families better, the FCSN board has established the Site Search Committee and the New Program Committee. Our East Bay adult day program has reached its capacity limit, so the Site Search Committee is in charge of looking for a new location. Since the new site may become our future headquarters, we are hoping to find a 15,000 to 20,000 square feet building in either Fremont or Milpitas. The New Program Committee is working on an adaptive skill training program which will aim to serve more severely disabled individuals. This is a new area we are exploring, and we have high hopes that it will be successful.

2020 has been a stressful year, to say the least. Please do your best to stay well and take care of yourself and your loved ones. Our staff and volunteers have worked very hard to make FCSN even better. With all the help we have, and all the effort we have put in, I believe 2021 will be a bright year for FCSN.

# FCSN SHINES AT DDS SYMPOSIUM

Johnna Laird (FCSN Newsletter Reporter and Editor),
Jan. 2021

FCSN was honored to be featured by California's Department of Developmental Services (DDS) among thousands of service providers in a fall 2020 four-segment symposium featuring outstanding alternative and innovative service providers for special needs children and adults during the pandemic.

Highlighting programs for children that FCSN has continued to provide, FCSN Executive Business Director Sylvia Yeh discussed: ASP, Enrichment Programs, and One-on One Flexible Subjects. For adults, Sylvia talked about ADP, SLS, ILS, SEP, TDS and transportation services. For families, Sylvia pointed out respite care, increased seminars, mentorships, family support and outreach, plus the new employment training program, Friends Coffee & Tea.

Sylvia also highlighted the new online tutoring program, launched with FCSN youth volunteers in response to pandemic; on-going enrichment programs that include the Lego Club and the Toastmasters' Club; a new student council launched during the pandemic; and a range of innovative classes, including cooking online, art instruction, current events, and language arts comprehension.

In the presentation which also involved Anna Wang, Sylvia emphasized the adaptability of FCSN's staff to learn new technology skills, to modify existing curriculum and innovate new courses and to begin offering five hours daily of day programming to FCSN clients after only two weeks of Shelter-in-Place.

Sylvia noted that FCSN staff made key decisions that contributed to success of programming during the pandemic, including: one Zoom link for each program, simplifying access for clients; breakout rooms to facilitate support at levels to meet client needs; freedom for clients to choose the classes they want to attend and have voice in classes that are offered; a range of platforms for clients to access; technological support including computers and hotspots for clients who need them; advance schedules sent to consumers and parents; and follow-up phone calls and in-person delivery of class materials tailored to clients' interests and skills.

DDS assigned FCSN a November 4 symposium presentation date, three days before FCSN's annual Gala. Sylvia recalls that she worked every night until midnight for two weeks straight. Sylvia used skills she was learning in the ten-week Train-the-Trainer classes, taught by high school student Eric Zhu to FCSN's staff to boost graphic art and design skills. Sylvia says it was exciting to have an immediate, real-world application of the skills.

DDS received more than 200 positive comments about FCSN's presentation. "The presentation provided confirmation that even a pandemic cannot stop us from adhering to our mission. We found a way to continue living our mission, providing services virtually," says Sylvia. "The positive comments were a pat on the shoulder for the work our staff is doing."

# SNTUTORING

## Hillary Chang (FCSN Voices Youth Reporter), Jan. 8, 2021

Since the launch of the SNTutoring (Special Needs Tutoring) program in March, the program has expanded from a pilot program with just thirteen students to more than 160 matches in just six months. The SNTutoring program, previously known as the Flexible Subject Virtual Tutoring Program, originated from a FCSN volunteer's concern about the effects of the shelter-in-place directive on special needs students.

When students first shifted to remote learning, many special needs students had their routines interrupted and daily activities stripped away. FCSN program coordinators agreed that a one-on-one tutoring program would offer structure in the students' daily lives and the specialized attention could make up for the disruption in their schedules.

As a result, FCSN Volunteer Manager Mannching Wang set up a month-long pilot program to test the idea. After the first thirteen students involved in the pilot program were surveyed, the program revealed a 100% percent satisfaction rate, with all parents interested in continuing with their matches. Due to the success of the pilot program, coordinators Linmei Chiao, Mannching Wang, Yvette Ying, and Isabella He developed the SNTutoring program with the mission of enriching the lives of FCSN students by fostering friendships between volunteer tutors and special needs students.

The SNTutoring program offers a year-round virtual program that supports students interested in a variety of academic and non-academic topics, ranging from STEM, drawing, and board games to music and sports. Among the program's most popular subjects are piano, reading, and math, which cumulatively account for more than 100 matches. Registrations are ongoing, and session dates and subjects are completely flexible – meaning the student's parents and the tutor can set up all logistics based on their own preferences. Once program coordinators discover a volunteer and a student with common interests, Tutor Coordinator Isabella He matches students and tutors together in the interest of forming life-long friendships. After a decided match, Parent Coordinator Yvette Ying connects the parents and tutors together, and the tutoring journey begins. What differentiates the program from other FCSN programs is the option for parents to tailor classes to their student's preferences. Parents often work with the tutor to customize classes to their child's learning abilities or interests, changing classes to match their child's learning abilities or degree of difficulty. Throughout the program, Program Supervisor Mannching Wang routinely performs check-ins by reviewing feedback forms from both parties to assure the quality of each session. Program Lead Linmei Chiao ensures that the program maintains its high-quality tutoring sessions and facilitates communications between coordinators, parents, and tutors.

Over the six months since the program began operation, the program has achieved a lot of success. The program coordinators have all received positive feedback from parents and students regarding the program. In fact, more than half of the students enjoy the program to such an extent that their parents have requested multiple tutors for their children.

The SNTutoring program's success lies in the youth volunteers' dedication and the students' eagerness to learn. With both parties' enthusiasm, volunteers and students have both heavily benefitted from the program. The program has enabled volunteers to form a bond with their students and witness their students grow session by session, as coordinator Isabella He explains, "the volunteering experience is one of the most meaningful experiences, because the bond [tutors] form is a direct bond that [they] can't really get at other programs and organizations." Similarly, the program has helped students remain socially active during the pandemic, while making up for the typical classes and in-person instructions students now lack. By establishing routine into the students' weekly schedules, the program brings more consistency back into their lives.

With all of the advancements in the SNTutoring program, program coordinators aim to carry on the program's mission of guiding FCSN students by teaching them how to build upon their strengths and improve every day, while also giving youth volunteers the opportunity to transform lives and witness steady growths in their students. As the program continues to grow, program coordinators are committed to tailoring sessions to accommodate the needs of each special needs student and strive to ensure each special needs student has the attention and support needed through his/her classes by following up more frequently on initial connections and hosting more regular check-ins. Program coordinators also work to improve the matching process by implementing an automated database to track matches more efficiently. Linmei Chiao said, "With such rapid growth within such a short time span, we hope to see many new faces join the program, along with the already familiar ones."

## Meet the program coordinators and hear their thoughts on the SNTutoring Program:

*I think we are a really good team. Everybody works together so well and we have different strengths and weaknesses. As the Co-Founder of FCSN, FCSN started in my living room, in my basement, in my house, so it is really natural for me to see all of these children as my children. For two years now, I have helped as the Director of the Volunteer Support Department of FCSN, so I gradually became inspired and touched from all of the volunteers – not only are the special needs students like my children – all of the volunteers are like my children too."*

## — Linmei Chiao, Program Lead

*My duties in the SNTutoring program are checking parents and tutors' feedback, supporting them, and making sure our students can benefit from this program. In order to make sure the tutoring quality is met, I will go to observe the classes, contact parents/volunteers, listen to their concerns, and try to meet their needs as much as possible. The happiest moment is when I see our special needs students building a strong bond with their tutors and the students and the tutors are both growing when they work together.*

## — Mannching Wang, Program Supervisor

*I cherish this opportunity because I get to know the parents and I get to see their names. I have another role as the Co-Director of the South Bay Enrichment program, where we are supposed to come up with meaningful lessons for the members. Occasionally I will see a demand that is not fulfilled by this SNTutoring program, so I can come up with a new idea for a group lesson or something similar so we can address that issue. This [program] really opened up my eyes so I can see the demands and see what is available, and I have used the volunteer talent bowl to to find teachers for new classes we offer, so it has been working well for me. I really enjoy this team, and I have been learning from everyone."*

**— Yvette Ying, Parent Coordinator**

*I would say working on this program is one of the most rewarding experiences I have had. Linmei, Mannching, and Yvette are the best team of coordinators I have ever worked with. Just seeing the appreciation from the parents and the students is very heartwarming. From the volunteers, I can see a lot of growth in terms of their volunteering and their experience with this program. A lot of my personal friends are also involved in this program, and they text me telling me how impactful the program has been on them and the bonds they have formed with their students have been incredible to see. It has just been very great being a program coordinator, and I am very thankful to be working on this program and seeing it grow.*

**— Isabella He, Tutor Coordinator**

# THE MAKING OF THE MUSIC VIDEO FOR FCSN 25TH ANNIVERSARY

James Chiao (FCSN Co-chair) & Hillary Chang (Youth Reporter), 2021

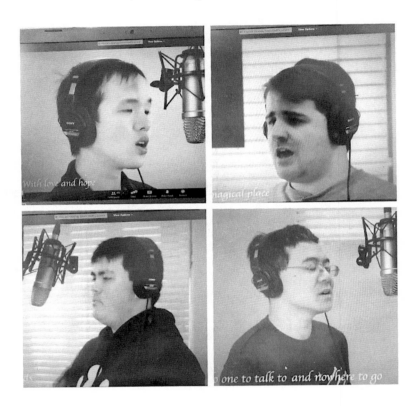

## How the Project Got Started

Tony Guo, a youth volunteer, first learned about FCSN from one of his close friends. He recalled, "My friend put in detail how to join FCSN on a Discord server. After I joined the Saratoga FCSN chapter, I heard that the FCSN 25th anniversary was coming up and they might need music to go along with a related project, so I asked my personal counselor at CP Mentorship, Catherine Liu, if she could help me connect to FCSN. To my surprise, she was actually closely connected with FCSN."

Catherine first got to know FCSN more than ten years ago. She went to a Special Needs Talent Showcase with her family and was very impressed. She went on to invite more friends to enjoy the event in the later years. Catherine spoke about the initiation of this project: "I have known Tony since he was an eighth grader in Redwood High School. Tony has been very into music, and he has also always had a big heart. I run a non-profit organization called CP Mentorship to help pair young children with mentors to do Impact Projects together. While talking to Tony about whom he wanted to help most during the pandemic, he mentioned FCSN. He is member of the FCSN club at Saratoga High. It has been almost a year since the lockdown, and he wants to help children with special needs in any way he could." Catherine then connected with Anna through Dean, her longtime friend and non-profit partner. Afterwards, Anna and Catherine started to brainstorm of possible projects for a high schooler who was interested in music/video production. From there, they came up with the idea of a song and a music video for FCSN's 25th anniversary

Catherine brought in Bruce Wenze Li to this project, who happens to be Tony's music teacher. Bruce is a music producer and music educator in the Bay Area. He has been working in the music industry for over ten years.

From the FCSN side, Anna invited Jim Chiao and Dora Chou to join this project. Anna served as the lead of the project, Dora helped coordinate the meetings and handle the logistics, and Jim helped with the lyrics, photo collection, and some coordination.

## Define the Music Video Project

The main goal of the music video project was to create an original song and a music video in celebration of FCSN's 25th anniversary. It was early March when the team first got together, and they decided that the theme of the song was to express FCSN's long term goal of building a community of love, hope, respect for our children with special needs. The schedule was fairly tight, as the team wanted to complete the music video by the end of May. Bruce had the most experience in music production, and he naturally became the director and producer of the music video.

In the first few meetings, Bruce laid out the steps of making a music video and his role in this project. Bruce explained, "For this project, my main responsibilities are to organize the whole project timeline and figure out the things we need to do, including composing music, writing lyrics, auditioning singer's, creating a recording schedule and a video shooting schedule, and many post-productions like music final mixing, video editing and color correction, etc. As a producer, I need to make sure the quality of the music and the video is good and the whole production is smooth. During the production, I will also teach Tony my experience of music producing. I think this is a good chance for everyone in this project to learn about music."

## Music Composition

Bruce had a complete production team behind him, and he was ready to supply all the resources from songwriting to singing and video production. He said that Tony Guo would work on the music composition first, and that needed to be done quickly. Tony did not disappoint us; he came back with the first version within two weeks. We all listened to it together at one Zoom meeting, it had a beautiful melody and was slow in tempo. Next, what the team needed was the lyrics.

## Writing the Lyrics

For the lyrics, FCSN team decided that it was best if they wrote it themselves – after all, no outsider could express their feelings better. To find people to write the lyrics, Jim first asked around the Board members and some parents. However, after one week without any response, Jim decided to take the matter into his own hands, even though he has never written any lyrics before. Separately, Anna asked parent writer, Johnna Laird, to write lyrics as well. Jim and Johnna each wrote their own pieces. However, they were not entirely satisfied, so they decided to work together. After two weeks, they got together with Anna, and finalized the lyrics during a long and exhaustive Zoom session.

Jim recalled: "In writing the lyrics, we want to talk about our special children, our mission, vision, and our Dream Project. However, it soon became clear that trying to express all these ideas in a few short lines was a huge challenge. Eventually, I remembered a Chinese article written by Sufen Wu many years ago with the title "Child of the Stars", and decided to write the song about the "Children of the Stars". At around the same time, Johnna also finished her version. As deadline approached, one night, Johnna, Anna, and I held a long Zoom meeting, and we combined the best parts of the two versions and hammered all the words into place. It was not easy, as the three of us argued over some lines and pondered over the use of some words. But we were relieved when it was all done, and it was truly a work of collaboration. As for the name of the song, we all liked Johnna's suggestion of *Friends of Dreams*, as it best describes many of us at FCSN."

## Finding the Singers

At first, Bruce thought of using outside singers. However, Anna insisted that the song be performed by our special needs individuals. She said that we have developed many talents at FCSN, and there is every reason to give them the opportunity to perform.

Anna explained, "I have fond memories of FCSN's first fund-raising gala in 2002 where our young children with special needs performed. Even though they were not polished performers, their cute and angelic faces stole the audience's hearts. Often, individuals with disabilities were looked upon as people with no abilities. It is FCSN's vision to change this mindset in the community. We have developed numerous programs and events to discover and develop our children's abilities and talent. Their journeys are all unique. They found their hidden gifts and passion at different ages, in their early years, in their teens, or even in their adulthood. On our 25th anniversary, we are proud to say that we've discovered and developed over 50 talented artists and performing artists within our BIG FCSN Family." Within two weeks, Anna was able to recruit six of FCSN's talented vocalists; and they are: Lawrence Wang, Greg Hebert, Frank Prenot, Andrew Quach, Michael Erhardt, and Tony Nakamoto. They were given a short time to practice before taping was to take place.

## Videotaping & Editing

The music video was taped over a weekend. Bruce recalled: "For video shooting, I think all the singers and parents did a really good job and it was way better than I expected. The whole process was smooth and all of the singers gave a pretty good performance. As a producer, I was really happy that we got all the footage in one shooting day."

He continued, "For the video editing part, the editor and I tried to line up all the perfect timing for the singers. We did the color correction and made sure it looked great. The addition of lyrics makes it easier for the audience to understand the song. Also, I would like to thank all the key crew members for their valuable feedback to make this music video better. I'm sure this is going to be a great memory for everyone."

## Final Thoughts

After the video was completed, Bruce added, "Music videos for me are a better way to let people understand the music or the song. For our project, of course, before we made the video, it was only a song with a beautiful melody and good voices. But after the video was released, people will know what is really happening to all the special needs people."

As a final thought, Catherine said, "I am very impressed with how capable these FCSN special needs individuals are. They have beautiful voices, confident smiles, and a very positive attitude towards everything they do. Also, I am amazed by how close the community is. I was initially puzzled why FCSN could attract so many volunteers each year. Now, after working with the community, I can understand why: FCSN is a source of energy and dreams."

They need a place

# Here are the lyrics and the link to the music video:

*They are children from the stars*
*Alone on Earth, going so far*
*No one to talk to*
*And nowhere to go*
*They need a magical place*
*To find their way*

*They need a place*
*Where they can shine*
*With love and hope*
*Is it their time?*
*We are Friends*
*To lend a hand*
*Changing the world*
*Every day*

*Touched by a magic wand*
*They find their wings*
*Bringing smiles, they start to sing*
*Flying high*
*Swaying 'n dancing*
*Dreams we've built*
*They are living*

*There's nothing*
*we can't do*
*Making dreams*
*come true*
*Love and hope*
*show the way*
*We are Friends*
*To lend a hand*
*Changing the world*
*Every day*

https://youtu.be/Ho6HLHwgPwg